THE LONG ROAD HOME

THE LONG ROAD HOME

THE RETURN OF THE EXILES FROM BABYLON TO ZION

A DEVOTIONAL COMMENTARY
ON THE BOOKS OF EZRA AND NEHEMIAH

A WEALTH OF SPIRITUAL INSIGHT INTO THE
GREATEST REVIVAL IN HISTORY

BY

SAMUEL T. CARSON

Author of "The Genesis Brides" "Desert House" and
"The Amazing Cross"

AMBASSADOR

Belfast Northern Ireland Greenville South Carolina

THE LONG ROAD HOME
© 1999 Samuel T. Carson

ISBN 1 84030 049 3

Ambassador Publications
a division of
Ambassador Productions Ltd.
Providence House
16 Hillview Avenue,
Belfast, BT5 6JR
Northern Ireland

Emerald House
1 Chick Springs Road, Suite 203
Greenville,
South Carolina 29609, USA
www.emeraldhouse.com

Contents

Part One
The Return Under Zerubbabel
To Build The House Of God
Ezra 1-6
page 7

Part Two
The Return Under Ezra
To Beautify The House Of God
Ezra 7-10
page 63

Part Three
The Return Under Nehemiah
To Build The City Of God
Nehemiah 1-13
page 99

Part One

The Return Under Zerubbabel

To Build The House of God

Ezra 1-6

INTRODUCTION *9*

Ezra chapter one
GREAT STIRRINGS *13*

Ezra chapter two
THE PIONEERS *22*

Ezra chapter three
MAKING A START *30*

Ezra chapter four
THE WORK IS STOPPED *38*

Ezra chapter five
STANDING AND WITHSTANDING *46*

Ezra chapter six
A GOOD FINISH *54*

INTRODUCTION

The book of Ezra begins where II Chronicles ends and the first two verses of the one book are identical to the last two verses of the other. In this way the writers emphasise the continuity of God's purposes. We must keep in mind, however, that between those two books lay a period of time which extended to some seventy years. That was the period of the Babylonian captivity, predicted with great precision by Jeremiah the prophet. "Thus saith the Lord, after seventy years are accomplished at Babylon, I will visit you, and perform my good word toward you, in causing you to return to this place." (Jer.29:10) This captivity should be carefully distinguished from the earlier captivity suffered by the northern kingdom. (See 2Kings 17:18.) Both captivities were Divine judgements upon a rebellious and disobedient people.

The seventy year captivity began in 606 B.C., and was completed in three stages. It was in the third year of King Jehoiakim that Judah was brought under servitude to the kingdom of Babylon. And then, in spite of the plainest warnings from Jeremiah that still greater judgement would overtake them should they refuse to acknowledge the hand of God in their situation, the people foolishly revolted against their Gentile masters.

This brought the army of Babylon against Jerusalem and led to the deportation of the people to the land of the Chaldeans. Only a token number were allowed to remain in their own land. But in a matter of a few months, and believing that help would come from Egypt, those who remained revolted yet again. This time the whole might of Babylon fell upon them, their land was laid waste and the great city of Jerusalem was destroyed. And so it was until 536 B.C. And then, when the seventy year period foretold by Jeremiah had run its course, God marvelleously turned the captivity of His people.

The Exiles Return

Among the first of the exiles carried into Babylon were Daniel and his three friends. The last chapter of II Chronicles is all about this carrying down to Babylon. But now, the captivity having run its course, the book of Ezra is the story of the captives' return to their homeland and to their holy city. Like the captivity itself, the return was also in three stages.

The purposes of God may at times seem to tarry but they cannot ever be thwarted, and they are never abandoned. The captivity was God's judgement on the chosen nation. It marked the end of the monarchy, for the time being at any rate. It signalled the total eclipse of Israel's power and prestige among the nations. Israel had become a by-word, no longer the head of the nations but the tail. The Times of the Gentiles had begun.

Nevertheless, the purposes of God go marching on for "none can stay His hand, or say unto Him, What doest thou?" (Dan.4:35) And so the captivity itself became a powerful instrument of Divine providence. It was used by God to prepare a remnant of the people to return to Zion. Even the timing of the return had the stamp of God upon it, for the recovery meant that the people were back in the land to herald the first advent of the promised Messiah. And in turn, this prepared the way for God's redemptive purposes to be realised.

Kingdoms rise and fall

Babylon and Nebuchadnezzar had shot their bolt and now the new and mightier empire of Persia had taken centre stage under Cyrus the Great. It is a most interesting detail, and one worthy of emphasis, that well over one hundred years before the captivity and the destruction of the Temple at Jerusalem, God had already identified this monarch by name, as the one who would decree the return of the people and the rebuilding of the Temple. (See Isa.44:28;45:1.) Because our God is omniscient, He knows all things, He is able to tell the end from the beginning. Things that we cannot see as yet, He can speak of as though they were already accomplished.

In the event, one of the first acts of the victorious Persian was to decree the return of the exiled people of God. This he did in 536 B.C. This meant that the way was now clear for the exiles to return and rebuild the house of their God which had been destroyed.

There have been times throughout the human story in which an overruling providence has manifested itself, and God has compelled the princes and rulers of this world to do His will. Such times often come when we are least aware of them, but in retrospect, we can only describe them as 'defining moments in history.'

The book before us witnesses, in a stirring way, to how God can and does overrule human designs and cause all things to work together according to His sovereign will, and for the furtherance of His purpose.

GREAT STIRRINGS

The six books of the kings describe the rise and the development of Israel, the chosen nation. They also trace the eventual division of that nation into two parts, a division that has not been healed to this day. They describe in some detail the failure, first of the northern kingdom, Israel, and then of the southern kingdom, Judah; and how God used the king of Assyria to judge the former and Nebuchadnezzar, king of Babylon, to judge the latter whose people he carried into captivity. Here, in the book of Ezra, we learn how, in the fulness of time, He used Cyrus the Persian as His chosen instrument to restore those same people from Babylon to their own land.

Some believe that the aged Daniel, prime minister in the administration of Cyrus, showed his monarch the earlier prophecies about the duration of the captivity. And it may well be that under God, Daniel's influence had the effect of disposing the king to be favourable towards the exiles. At the same time the Jewish historian, Josephus, says that Cyrus read the book of Isaiah himself. And when he came to the part where Isaiah mentioned him by name, "an ambition and an earnest desire seized him to fulfil what was written."

There may be truth in both reports but, whatever the reality, we cannot overlook the fact that the living God often takes up the most unlikely characters and uses them in the accomplishment of His grand designs. He used His people to judge the Amorite nations that were in Canaan in Joshua's day and, then, when His people apostatised He used those same Amorite nations as a scourge to judge His people. And in the story before us He actually calls both Nebuchadnezzar, king of Babylon and Cyrus, king of Persia His servants.

The Recovery Begins

The first stage of the three stages in the return to Zion was led by Zerubbabel who was a descendant of David's royal house. Although this book bears the name of Ezra, Ezra himself does not feature in it until chapter seven, where we find him leading the second stage of the recovery. The first six chapters are all about the experiences of the exiles who returned under Zerubbabel. They were the pioneers of the recovery.

Spiritually, life in these two centres, Zion or Jerusalem and Babylon, speak to us of two different kinds or levels of life that may be experienced by the people of God at any given time. It was always up to Zion and down to Babylon. (Note how often the word up occurs in this book.) Paul identified the spiritual significance of these places when he charged the Corinthian believers, "I could not speak unto you as unto spiritual but as unto carnal." (1Cor.3:1) Here we have life on two entirely different planes and here we have the New Testament counterparts of Zion and of Babylon.

Corinth was the carnal church of Paul's day. The members of that church could not receive any doctrine worthy to be described as meat. Their only capacity was for milk. There is, of course, nothing wrong with milk, but milk is for babes. These people had not matured so as to be able to receive solid food and as a result they were marked by such things as envy and strife and division. They were man centred when they should have been God centred and Christ centred. On all these grounds they were manifesting the marks of the carnal man. Spiritually, they were like the people of old by the rivers of Babylon.

How Christians may lapse into the carnal state is illustrated in the circumstances that led to the captivity in Babylon. As already noted, the books immediately preceding the book of Ezra reveal how the once great kingdom of David and Solomon had become "a people scattered and peeled." Those books record the lamentable tale of how the utter failure of the chosen people themselves, eventually led to the break up of the kingdom and ultimately, to their own captivity.

Why the Captivity took place

The scriptures highlight two causes for the decline and fall of the theocratic kingdom. First, love for the Lord had grown cold and, secondly, idolatry had usurped the place that should have been the Lord's in the hearts and minds of His people. The whole law is summed up in the words, 'You shall love the Lord your God with all your hearts,' and, 'You shall have no other gods before me.' Quite clearly these ideals no longer prevailed.

Ezekiel bore graphic witness to this when, transported in spirit back to Jerusalem, he beheld the departing of the shekinah, the glory cloud, that covered the first temple. He was permitted, at that time, to see the inner workings of Judaism and it was not an edifying sight. He saw the idolatry carried on in the house of God, and actually carried on alongside the formal maintenance of the usual temple services. (See Ezekiel Chs.8-12.)

And then there was the second cause; the word of God had been seriously neglected. For four hundred and ninety years the ordinance governing the use of the land had been set aside. Every seven years the land was to enjoy a sabbath. For that whole year the land was to be rested; there was to be no ploughing, no sowing and no harvesting. But seventy times seven years had passed and this ordinance had not been observed. And then came the captivity which lasted for seventy years so that the land might at last enjoy those neglected sabbaths.

These two root causes of the captivity have their spiritual counterpart to-day. The decline of these two things, love for the Lord and obedience to His word, has reduced the whole tone of our Christian experience and led us, spiritually, down to Babylon when all the while we should be living on the higher plane. Jesus said, "If you love me keep my commandments." And every heart that truly loves the Saviour's Name will surely be marked by an attitude of subjection to the Lord Himself and to His word.

We have already cited Corinth as a sharply drawn and very pertinent lesson. Quite plainly, the Lord no longer had the central place in Corinth and this resulted in a state of carnality which made that church a reproach to the worthy name of Jesus. It is easy to dismiss things of this nature as being of no relevance to us in our day, but they were written for our instruction, that we might be warned. May we ponder them deeply and never fail to examine ourselves in the light of them.

People made willing

How the recovery from Babylon began is also deeply instructive. The Lord stirred up the spirit of Cyrus, king of Persia, to make a proclamation and put it in writing, saying, "The Lord God of heaven has charged me to build Him a house in Jerusalem, which is in Judah. Who is there among you of all His people? The Lord, his God, be with him, and let him go up." (II Chron.36:23) This proclamation had the effect of fulfilling the word God had spoken through Isaiah the prophet some two hundred years before. "He shall let go my captives, ... saying to Jerusalem, Thou shalt be built." (See Isa.44:28,45:13.)

"And then the Lord stirred up the spirit of Zerubbabel...and the spirit of all the remnant of the people...and they came and did work in the house of the Lord of hosts, their God." (Hag.1:14) What marvellous stirrings there were in those days; stirrings of which God Himself was the instigator. The exiles sensed that prayer was being answered and that the thing they longed to see was coming to pass. (See Psa.137:1.) This moved them to action and the leaders of the people, of Judah and Benjamin, and the priests and the Levites, stirred themselves up and their hands were strengthened by the support they were given by others. (See Ezra 1:5.)

When the Tabernacle was under construction, in Moses' time, the people rallied to their leaders and made available to them all that it was within their power to give, so that the work of God might prosper. And now, once again, the people rallied and gave according to their ability. Nor did they give grudgingly, for the record clearly states that, as in that earlier day, all that was given was willingly offered.

We find the same patterns in the histories of the great spiritual revivals that have occurred from time to time since the inception of the Christian church. Willing hearted and open handed giving was certainly very much in evidence in western lands, during the revival of 1859. Occasionally tidings still reach us of similar stirrings today, mainly from less favoured eastern lands. The need for such manifestations of God's presence, in grace and power, presses itself upon every truly exercised soul. The need is especially urgent throughout the western world where materialism has come to reign supreme.

Oh for the floods on a thirsty land,
Oh for a mighty revival;
Oh for a sanctified fearless band,
Ready to hail its arrival.

There are two commonly accepted views on revival. One was expressed by Charles Finney, the well known American revivalist of a former age. He said, "Fulfil God's conditions, and you will have God's blessing." The other view was expressed by the saintly Samuel Rutherford, of Scotland. Standing by the shore one day when the tide was out, he said, "What can I do to bring the tide in? Nothing! I must wait God's time, and then the tide will come in."

Both views are correct but neither of them is balanced. Scripture says, "You have need of patience that, after you have done the will of God, you might receive the promise." (Hebs.10:36) It is ours to stir ourselves, and so to brace ourselves to do the will of God; but then, having done that, we must still wait God's time. True revival is nothing less than God Himself moving in a sovereign way, by His Spirit, in the midst of His people.

This is what happened at the time of the recovery from Babylon. God's clock had struck, His purposes were ripening fast. God was moving towards the bringing in of the promised Messiah and the ultimate accomplishment of His redemptive purposes. All this required that the chosen people should be present in the promised land. This is what gave urgency to the leaders and to the people to stir themselves up. They assuredly gathered that the Lord was in this matter. And those who able to do so gave of their material things and thus they too helped forward the recovery.

It has to be said that only a remnant of the people were of one heart and one mind to return to Zion. These had often sat by the rivers of Babylon and wept and said, "If I forget thee, O Jerusalem, let my right hand forget her cunning; if I do not remember thee, let my tougue cleave to the roof of my mouth." (Psa 137:5,6) And now, conscious of a Divine intervention in their behalf, they were determined to move forward in fellowship with the Lord.

But not all were ready to leave Babylon. Jerusalem and its temple lay in ruins and held no attraction for many. A great number had grown comfortable in Babylon and preferred to remain there. It is not difficult to see parallels between those days and our own. Over against the great masses of nominal people throughout professing

Christendom how few there are who are ready to bear the reproach of Christ.

The Vessels of the House of God

Seventy years before, Nebuchadnezzar had plundered the Temple in Jerusalem, he had looted the holy vessels and placed them in the house of his gods in Babylon. In his tradition he was showing that his own gods were greater than the gods to whom those vessels had been dedicated, greater even than Jehovah. Later, these precious vessels were to be defiled by Belshazzar on the very night that the city was taken by the armies of the Medes and Persians.

But now the time had come for Jehovah to make bare His arm and show Himself strong in the behalf of His people. He began by moving Cyrus to bring forth the holy vessels and to entrust them to one called Sheshbazzar. The vessels were numbered into his hand before he left Babylon; and when the convoy reached Jerusalem the vessels were numbered out of his hand. Throughout the long journey Sheshbazzar was responsible to maintain the integrity of this sacred trust.

Paul speaks of believers as being vessels in the Lord's house. "In a great house there are not only vessels of gold and silver, but also of wood and of earth; and some to honour, and some to dishonour. If a man, therefore, purge himself...he shall be a vessel unto honour, sanctified, and fit for the master's use, and prepared unto every good work." (2Tim.2:20,21.) There was, of course, great variety among the temple vessels committed to Zerubbabel but all were alike precious to the Lord.

As we go through this book we shall find many references to these vessels. At this point we might simply note that the listed vessels in this first chapter numbered around 2,499 (v.9,10) whereas the total number of vessels was 5,400. (v.11) The difference between the two figures is easily explained by the fact that there were many other vessels besides those specifically identified. In one of our Lord's miracles, the 5 loaves and the 2 fishes seem to be precise numbers; but the number who were fed seems to be imprecise, for in addition to the men, there were also women and children. Many other examples could be cited of this use of numbers in scripture.

Zerubbabel - God's man for the hour

We should also note that the mysterious person named Sheshbazzar the prince of Judah seems to have been none other than Zerubbabel, although thought by some to have been Nehemiah. (See ch.2:2.) It appears to have been normal practice in Babylon to take away from the captives their Hebrew names and to give them Babylonian names instead. Daniel and his three friends are notable examples of this and are familiar to us. (See Dan.1:6,7.) The same thing appears to have happened to Zerubbabel whose name means stranger in Babylon. And so, when the holy vessels were handed over to him by a representative of the government, his Babylonian name was used.

This means that for the first time in scripture we are introduced to this remarkable character who played such a crucial role in the recovery of God's people and in their return to Zion. Zerubbabel is one of those Old Testament characters who serve as types of Christ, and it is most profitable to view him in that way. The most immediate thing to be said about him is that he was totally subject to the word of the Lord. He believed God and obeyed His word.

Two of the three post-exilic prophets, Haggai and Zechariah, exercised their ministry in the time of Zerubbabel. It seems probable that they were among the exiles who returned with him to Jerusalem. Malachi was another prophet who came a little later. He was to Nehemiah, what the others had been to Zerubbabel.

Several times in the book of Haggai we read how the word of the Lord came to Zerubbabel through the prophet. (See Hag.1:1. 2:1,2. 3:20,21.) We also read of the response made to that word. "Then Zerubbabel...and Joshua...with the remnant of the people, obeyed the voice of the Lord, their God, and the words of Haggai, the prophet, as the Lord their God, had sent him." (Hag.1:12) Zerubbabel surely pointed forward to the coming one who could say, "My meat is to do the will of Him who sent me."

This simple and uncomplicated submission to God's word was another mark of the genuineness of the great stirrings of heart among the people in Babylon as the captivity drew to a close. God was at work. The Lord had spoken, and all the earth must keep silent before Him.

Zerubbabel also benefited from the ministry of Zechariah. "This is the word of the Lord unto Zerubbabel, saying, Not by might, nor by power, but by my Spirit, says the Lord of hosts." (Zech.4:6) Zerubbabel had great authority; originally he received it from Cyrus and later it was confirmed by Darius, but there was also a higher power, and in that the confidence of this great leader rested. What was the combined power of those two illustrious monarchs of great Persia in comparison to the power of the Most High God, the possessor of heaven and earth?

But let us hear from Zechariah once more, "The word of the Lord came unto me, saying, The hands of Zerubbabel have laid the foundation of this house; his hands shall also finish it." (Zech.4:8,9) Doubtless, some of these words were spoken during the latter part of Zerubbabel's life, but we learn from the inspired records that they were fulfilled to the letter. Zerubbabel went forward, in dependence upon God and in obedience to His word, and he proved the faithfulness of God. The Lord demonstrated Himself to be faithful to His word, for in the end, the hands of Zerubbabel finished the work and God was glorified.

Nor must we lose sight of the fact that the return of this remnant foreshadows the return of scattered Israel to the land of promise in the last days. That future return will be just as real and literal as the return of the exiles so long ago. But in that day, a greater than Zerubbabel will go before His people. The Lord Himself shall be their ensign and unto Him shall the gathering of the people be.

ThE PioneerS

There are several chapters in the Bible like Ezra chapter two. At first sight they seem to be nothing more than lists of names, lists of numbers etc. But there are many good reasons why these chapters should have been included in the sacred canon. For instance, sometimes we come upon an issue in scripture that seems shrouded in mystery; and then we discover a reference in one of these chapters that acts like a key and enables us to unlock the secret.

Or again, we sometimes come across a passage like the chapter before us that seems to be an unrelieved series of rather stuffy, gloomy facts, and then, just as we are about to give up our study of them, we discover a gem that makes all our effort well worthwhile. An example of this is seen in the first such chapter in the Bible. (Genesis Five) In that chapter one and another is said to have lived, and then died. But reading on we come to Enoch, and the amazing things said about him. At that point the history is so different, we are constrained to pause, and in doing so, we may learn how Enoch graphically illustrates the true hope of every true believer in Jesus Christ.

God has His Records

Now God has His records, He has a book of remembrance (Mal 3:16), and we know that when the time for judgement comes the books will be opened. This must be true for His people at the Judgement Seat as it will be for unbelievers at the Great White Throne. These chapters, such as the one now before us, which we are tempted to pass over lightly should be viewed as sample pages from those divine records.

In a curious way they remind us that "God is not unrighteous to forget our work and labour of love, which we have showed toward His name, in that we have ministered to the saints and do minister." (Hebs.6:10) They set forth the kind of things that God takes note of, and they teach us that when it comes to things that are of lasting value, God's thoughts are often different from our own.

The chapter before us is the register of the names of those who went up with Zerubbabel in the first phase of the return from captivity. Beginning with the leaders the list works right down the line. The recovery was not a solo enterprise, it was a corporate business. Among the leaders, who went up before the people were Jeshua and Nehemiah. The former was the High Priest of that day. He was a man who understood priestly ministry. We make much in theory of the priesthood of all believers, but in practical terms, how much do we know about the ministry of today's believer-priests?

Nehemiah, (not be confused with the great reformer of whom we read in the next book) appears only this once in the sacred canon. But if he lived up to the meaning of his name, what a help he must have been. His name means, 'the Lord's encourager'. He must have been fully employed throughout the long journey from Babylon to Jerusalem. The church always has need for people of this calibre. May many be raised up among us in our generation.

The reference in the final verse of this chapter to all Israel should be noted. Here and elsewhere in the book the totality of the chosen nation is maintained. It was the people of Judah who were carried into Babylon but the recovery included representatives of all the tribes. We become sectarian when we allow ourselves to become so absorbed in our own little group that we lose sight of the body of Christ. We must always have the larger picture before us and at all times endeavour to keep the unity of the Spirit in the bond of peace.

It would be a burdensome task to try and analyse each of the groups that followed those leaders back to Zion. Members of families, of the priesthood and of the Levites etc. are all listed. Together they teach us that all His people are known to God, and that He takes note of them who do justly, love mercy, and walk humbly with their God. These pages teach the precious truth that such are before Him in perpetual remembrance and that He does not forget the least. He marks faithfulness and assures us that it will not be without its reward.

Those who returned

We are only able to note some of the more salient details of this inspired page. For instance, what stands out clearly is that some of these families would have been expected to take part in the return from the captivity. Bethlehem was the city of David, and the children of Bethlehem were there. (v.21) And the men of Anathoth, Jeremiah's home town, were there. (v.23) It is interesting to note how God told beforehand the awful judgement upon Anathoth because of its antipathy towards Jeremiah. It would appear that having judged those sinners, God raised up in their stead a generation of righteous men. (See Jer.11:21-23.)

On the other hand, some were there whom we might not have expected. For instance, there were twice as many from Jericho, as there were from Bethel and Ai combined. (vv 28,34) Moreover, the Levites were conspicous by their small number. They numbered only seventy-four. The Levites were outnumbered ten to one by the priests, and they were also considerably outnumbered by the Singers. Later, we shall find that Ezra too was troubled by the small number of Levites in his party. Who can deny that all this has its parallel in the story of the Christian church.

Take any local fellowship, and what do we find? We sincerely rejoice to see those present who come from a gospel background and who have known the Holy Scriptures from childhood. But what delight it gives us to see others who have been plucked from a wholly godless past, now taking their place among the redeemed of the Lord. Indeed, by their zeal for the Lord the latter often put the former to shame.

God is sovereign and His grace is free. The gospel is a fruitful vine whose branches run over the wall. We should never limit God or put constraints upon His grace. We should always rejoice when Christ is preached, even where this is done out of envy and strife, and not out of love and good will. (Phil.1:15) And in the fellowship of His people we must ever be ready to find a place for all who love our Lord Jesus Christ in sincerity. Too much division has been the result of differences, the pettiness of which sadly reflect an appallingly low spiritual state.

The children of Solomon's servants

Twice over we read of the children of Solomon's servants. (vv 55,58) Some consider these references to refer to the descendants of those from outside Israel whom Solomon employed in the building of the first temple. (1Kings 5:13) Solomon, of course, is a type of Christ risen and glorified. It might be helpful, and perhaps not too out of place, to think of Solomon's servants in terms of those whom the Lord has called to leave their secular employment and to spend their whole time in His service.

We should pray for the offspring of such, recognising the peculiar temptations that often confront them. Should such go astray the adversary is very ready to point the accusing finger and the fellowship to which they had been attached can also be embarrassed. Worse still, the parents, whose personal godliness may be above reproach, can become seriously weakened and demoralised and may even be knocked out of the battle altogether.

Hanna, the mother of the prophet Samuel, was a woman of prayer and her son became a man of prayer. In times of difficulty, the people would come to him and say, "Pray for us." And in complete sincerity, Samuel could reply, "God forbid, that I should sin against the Lord, in ceasing to pray for you." But Samuel's offspring were not up to the standard of their father's godliness, and this must have been a grief to their father and a great source of weakness in Israel. (See 1Sam.8:1-5.) But such a situation is not unique to Samuel, it has been repeated over and over again. Pray for the children of Solomon's servants.

Singing the Lord's Song

We have already noticed the presence of the singers. They surely savoured the occasion and they must have played a full part in it. They would have recalled the times of weeping as they sat by the rivers of Babylon and hung their harps on the willows. But now as they led the praise of the returning remnant and came to Zion with singing and with everlasting joy upon their heads, they must have had the ancient prophecies before their minds. (See Isa.35:10.)

Their theme song was known as 'The Lord's Song', so called because its one grand theme was the Lord Himself. Theirs was a strain of music that identified them as belonging to the Lord. In this they have much to teach us to-day. In the assembly of His people our singing should be like theirs, it should be a making melody in our hearts unto the Lord. They must have sung the Lord's song with great delight and their refrain was, 'They shall obtain joy and gladness, and sorrow and sighing shall flee away.' (See Psa.137:1-4. Isa.35:10.)

Doubtful Cases

But some presented themselves whose title to be there was not clear. (vv 61-63) They did have a pedigree of sorts but its validity was in some doubt. These were handled with great care, because weakness would result if those who did not belong were mixed in among the true Israel of God. Sadly, it would seem that many in the

Christian profession to-day occupy that position. For whatever reason, many are found among the saints who are like the tares among the wheat. The very great caution exercised by Zerubbabel in dealing with these people is a timely warning to all responsible Christian leaders.

The presence of such people now, as then, can only have a debilitating effect upon the testimony. Inevitably they will develop a chip on the shoulder, if not on both shoulders. They will become discontented and eventually disillusion will set in. The effect may be that the whole assembly will also become disaffected and may even be divided. They will come to reflect the character of the mixed multitude who murmured against Moses. Having failed to gain Canaan, they resented that they had actually lost Egypt in the attempt.

Receiving new members into the church of God is always a heavy responsibility. If people are received who have no real right to be there, they are being put into a false position. And for such unfortunate people disastrous consequences can follow, consequences that may reach beyond time and into eternity. Solomon, in his day, made shields of gold to hang in the Temple at Jerusalem. His successor, Rehoboam, substituted shields of brass. The latter, when polished up, looked good, but they were only an imitation of the real thing. We need to learn, over and over again, the lesson of the Temple shields.

But if this situation had great potential to enfeeble the people, there was great faithfulness as well. Zerubbabel, the Governor, (A.V. Tirshatha) urged caution, at least, until such times as their title might be established. It may be that he was mindful of that mixed multitude that had come out of Egypt with Moses, and so his counsel was that a judgement respecting these people required a definite waiting upon God for as long as it took to discern His mind. The Urim and the Thummim were the divinely appointed provision for discerning the mind of the Lord in matters of this nature. (See Ex.28:30.)

People and their Possessions

Another thing that might be noted in this remarkable chapter is that God not only takes account of His people, He takes account of their possessions as well. In those days wealth was counted in terms of cattle and camels etc. (See vv 64-67.) The principle, however, is no different to-day for God still challenges His people about their possessions. "Will a man rob God? Yet you have robbed me. But you say, Wherein have we robbed you? In tithes and offerings." (Mal.3:8)

Believers should "Honour the Lord with their substance, and with the firstfruits of all their increase." (Prov.3:9) The repeated appeals for money and the fund raising gimmicks sponsored by the professing church must stink in the nostrils of the Almighty. While in the eyes and ears of a Godless world the sorry sight must be a constant source of reproach. For God's work to command God's blessing it must be done in God's way.

The Christian position regarding material things, is that we must hold all that comes our way as stewards, knowing that one day we will render an account of our stewardship. It is a solemn prospect, that when the books are opened at the Judgement Seat of Christ, our stewardships will be passed under review. May we each have the Master's commendation for faithfulness and may we not be ashamed in that day when we stand before Him.

A striking example of faithfulness in this matter is given in the closing verses of our chapter. "Some, when they came to Jerusalem, offered freely for the house of God. They gave after their ability into the treasury of the work." (vv. 68,69) The whole multitude must have been tremendously encouraged by this unsolicited bounty. Those who gave were heads of families. Leading by example,- they put themselves in a powerful position to call forth the very best in others.

That Sacred Place

When the exiles arrived in Jerusalem they made their way at once to the very place where God had chosen to put His name. It does not say that they came to the ruins, although the Temple was in ruin, but they came to the house of the Lord. In spite of everything, that house still existed in the mind of God and in the hearts of His people. They loved that spot. It was the spot where the fathers had worshipped the Lord and now the exiles had returned to witness a marvelleous restoration of that same worship in that very same place.

The final verse of the chapter also makes reference to people called the Nethinim. It is difficult to be dogmatic about who they were. Many believe they were descendants of the Gibeonites whom Joshua received without enquiring of the Lord and whom he appointed as hewers of wood and drawers of water for the congregation. (See Josh. 9:27.) Later, David appointed them to help the Levites in their service. And after the exile they became known as 'ministers of the house of God.'

It seems that following an uncertain start the Nethinim eventually found an established place among God's people and in the end, it would appear that their zeal outshone even the zeal of those they had been appointed to help. How often this strange scenario has been re-enacted in local churches. Let us be reserved in our judgements of others and let us be patient with those who are weak and who at the beginning seem to falter. And let us especially look to ourselves that no man takes our crown.

Making A Start

The third chapter begins with the activities of the returned remnant during the seventh month (their Tisri, our October) of that first year of freedom. The seventh month was, of course, the month of the feasts of Trumpets and Tabernacles.(v.4) Both these feasts look forward to a still future and final regathering of Israel, long foretold by the prophet Isaiah. (See Isa.11:11.) The return of the exiles under Zerubbabel was a foretaste of what shall be in that day when God will gather together the outcasts of Israel and the dispersed of Judah from every tribe and nation and bring them again to the land of promise.

The captivity itself had signalled a sea change in international politics. As we have already noted, political power in the earth had passed into Gentile hands. The 'Times of the Gentiles' had begun. The centre and seat of government in the earth had moved away from Jerusalem. This meant that whereas before the captivity Judah had been an independent kingdom, it was now just a province of the Persian Empire. Zerubbabel and his people were certainly living in a period of international upheaval, a period marked by profound and far reaching change.

The Oneness of the people

Before we consider the things to which they gave priority upon their return to Jerusalem, we must look at the more general scene described in this chapter. The people gathered themselves together as one man. (v.1) Then we read how they stood together, (v.9) and finally, how they worshipped together. (v.11) That is how it was, the many were as one. They gathered together, they stood together and they worshipped together.

In a day when the fragmentation of the Christian testimony is in fashion and has already reached alarming proportions, it is not difficult to discern here vital lessons for ourselves. First, there is a reminder of how things were with the church at the beginning. "They were all with one accord in one place." (Acts 2:1) And then there is the record of how believers were commanded from the beginning, to "Forsake not the gathering of themselves together." We are also told to love one another, to be kind one to another and to bear one another's burdens and so fulfil the law of Christ. It should hardly be necessary, therefore, to emphasise the corporate, the one another, nature of both the body of Christ and the local church

Christian believers are not just a collection of individuals, we are members one of another for we are members together in the body of Christ. We give expression to this by meeting together locally for fellowship, for prayer and for the breaking of bread. These gatherings in turn should be brief and hallowed foretastes of the great gathering that shall be at the coming again of our Lord. The complete and public manifestation of our oneness awaits the Lord's return, for only then shall "we all come in the unity of the faith unto a perfect man, unto the measure...of the fulness of Christ." (Eph.4:13)

Ecumenism is a subject that has been much debated in recent years. There is a false ecumenism and all who seek to be faithful to the Lord will be wary of it. But there is also a true and Biblical ecumenism and a solemn duty is laid upon those who are the Lord's to preserve and promote it. Here is how it was created. The unifying Baptism of the Spirit took place at Pentecost, and every believer partakes of that baptism at the point of conversion, and so the people of God are made one body in the Lord, they are one in Christ.

In the meantime, while we wait for God's Son from heaven, we must "endeavour to keep the unity of the Spirit in the bond of peace." (Eph.4:3) It has to be admitted that we are not very good at this, and our failure at this point has brought much reproach upon our Saviour's name. The returned exiles have important lessons to teach us in this matter. What they did in that seventh month is a timely reminder to us that where the Holy Spirit is at work the people of God are always drawn together. The Spirit always unites the saints.

This is a particularly crucial matter for the leaders of God's people. Divisions manifesting themselves in the church are very often a reflection of existing and perhaps long standing divisions among the overseers, elders and deacons. When contentious issues arise if those appointed to leadership in the church would only wait more upon God, He would surely cause them to be of one mind. And then, in turn, the mass of believers would be emboldened to stand together, and should the enemy 'put his most dreadful forms, of rage and mischief on' they will be found still standing, victorious on the field of battle.

They also worshipped together. And the Christian church is nothing at all, if it is not a worshipping community. Indeed, only in this character can the church realise its potential and fulfil its mission in the world. With insight it has been said that the Son came seeking sinners, but now the Father comes seeking worshippers. "The true worshippers shall worship the Father in spirit and in truth; for the Father seeks such to worship Him." (John 4:23)

Alas, the whole concept of worship has been devalued to such a degree, that this highest exercise of the human spirit has been reduced, in some quarters, to a session of noisy chorus singing and in others to a listless, lifeless singing of traditional hymns without any heart involvement in the exercise. A sense of meaningfulness needs to be rediscovered in the corporate worship of the church. In the returned remnant at Jerusalem, we have a beautiful illustration of what every fellowship of believers should be. Gathered together and standing together they also worshipped together.

The Word of God

It is of more than passing interest to note the place the returned captives gave to the word of God. In offering burnt offerings, they did so, "as it is written in the law of Moses, the man of God." (v.2) And in observing the feast of tabernacles, it was "as it is written." (v.4) And then, when they laid the foundation of the second temple, the accompanying ceremonial was "after the ordinance of David, king of Israel." (v.10)

One thing that the history of revival teaches, is that every new work that endured was founded on the word of God. The revivals of Hezekiah's day and of Josiah's day are evidence of this. On the other hand, every new work that faltered was usually weak at this point. Where God finds an obedient heart He will always give the needed grace and power to walk in the light of His word. True recovery always brings believers back to a new and fresh appreciation of the Word of God.

It is still true, "Everyone who hears these sayings of mine and does them is like a man who builds his house on a rock. And everyone who hears these sayings of mine and does them not, is like a man who builds his house on the sand." (See Matt.7:24-27.) Neglect of that word was one of the root causes of their captivity; and now upon their return the exiles were determined to give that very word its proper place of authority.

Important Priorities

It is well worth noting the two things they attended to first when they came to Jerusalem. They set up the altar of God. (v.2,3) And then they set forward the house of God. (v.10) The altar in question was the altar of burnt offering which invariably speaks of consecration and devotion with special reference to the person of the Lord Jesus. The place they accorded the altar reminds us of Paul's exhortation, "That in all things He must have the pre-eminence." (Col.1:18) "Lovest thou me?" is still the supreme question. To be able to answer this question in a positive way should be normative for the Christian.

Underlying all that they did was a certain fear. "Fear was upon them because of the people of those countries." (v.3) This does not seem to have been the fear of cowardice, for they were not lacking in courage, certainly not at that point in the story. On the contrary it was a godly fear. They were probably mindful of the idolatry into which the nation had fallen and which had become the occasion of their captivity, and now they were afraid in case the same thing should overtake them once again.

It was through neglect of the altar that idolatry had gained a foothold in the first instance. Their present purpose was to prevent the same failure repeating itself. It has to be significant that whatever other failures may have overtaken the Jewish people over the years since the captivity, idolatry was not one of them. By the rivers of Babylon they had time to repent of their idolatry and to turn from it. Idolatry, like covetousness, is very pernicious and the message of what they did at the first should at least be clear to us, the best resource against evil is to take our stand openly and emphatically on the Lord's side. The altar of devotion to Christ must be maintained.

And then, the second priority is spelt out; they set forward the house of God. (v.10) Now this brings before us the wonderful truth of Christ mystical. The house of God to-day is a spiritual house, but in that day it was material. To-day's spiritual house is made up of living stones, all of whom are built upon 'the Living Stone' - the risen Christ Himself. Our house of God is the church, expressed locally in that fellowship of believers with which the Lord has led us to identify ourselves.

If Jesus Christ is pre-eminent, and if we are to serve Him in any useful way, we must have some understanding of His present purpose. To Simon Peter and the other disciples He said, "I will build my church..." and He has adhered to that purpose ever since. For our part, as we seek to advance the upbuilding of His church we become labourers together with. And the best way to achieve this goal is to labour for the upbuilding of our own local church.

Taken together these two priorities clearly suggest that love for Christ Himself and love for His people are the essential distinguishing marks of the true Christian. The former identifies the primary object of our affections and the latter the way in which this is to be expressed. If in the first place the love of Christ constrains us then we shall be mindful of His own word "By this shall all men know that you are my disciples, that you have love one to another." (John 13:35)

Had the returned exiles been guided by worldly wisdom, the probability is that they would have been more interested in erecting fortifications of one kind or another to protect themselves from the hostile nations surrounding them. But their trust was in the God whose overruling hand had so amazingly preserved them in Babylon and now had protected them on their long journey back to Jerusalem. At last they had their priorities right and the meaning of those priorities should be pondered by us all.

Gift and Service

A very beautiful scene is now brought before us. The workmen had their work to do and so had the priests and the Levites, as well as all the people. Together they did what they had to do and the blessing of the Lord was upon them. We know that service for God is always according to divine gift. We also know that while some have been endowed with many gifts, and others with few, the Spirit of God has not left a single believer without some gift to enable him or her to serve God. He has "divided to everyone severally according to His will." (1Cor.12:11)

But the real question is seldom one of enablement or even of opportunity, it is rather one of faithfulness in the presence of opportunity. There is joy in serving the Lord and every Christian should be alert to the opportunities for service that abound on every hand. The question which one of his entourage put to Naaman the leper was this, "If the prophet had bid you do some great thing, would you not have done it?" Many empty handed Christians seem to be waiting for the Lord to give them 'some great thing' to do.

However, both scripture and experience teach that it is by being faithful in that which is least that we are then entrusted with some larger service. The people of the remnant will surely rise in judgement against this generation and condemn it. For some of them could only shout, and that is precisely what they did, and God was glorified. This principle was underlined in Jesus' ministry when He insisted that everything done in the Lord's name, even down to the giving of a cup of cold water in His name, would have its reward. (See Matt.10:42.)

Besides the shouts of those who shouted for joy on that memorable occasion, there was also the weeping of those who remembered the grandeur of the earlier temple of Solomon. In fact, the shouting and the weeping were so intermingled, one could not be distinguished from the other. Yet the reasons for both were plainly seen. Some who remembered the first temple considered what they now beheld so insignificant all they could do was to weep.

The weeping was by the older people and while they may have felt justified in their attitude, dwelling in the past can be counter productive. It can have the effect of paralysing the present and of discouraging those who are sincerely seeking to do something for God. By all means let us learn from the past and build upon it. But let us be careful in case the past causes us to undervalue the present. After all, the second temple was destined to be dignified in a way the first had never been. It was dignified by the personal presence of God Himself in human flesh (John 2:13,14).

And we should not overlook the fact that the people who shouted for joy, by their shouting, actually fulfilled the word of God given by the mouth of Jeremiah. "Thus says the Lord, Again there shall be heard in this place, which you say shall be desolate...in the cities of Judah and in the streets of Jerusalem...the voice of joy, and the voice of gladness; the voice of the bridegroom, and the voice of the bride; the voice of them who shall say, Praise the Lord of hosts; for the Lord is good; for His mercy endureth forever." (Jer.33:10,11) Regrets over the past can indeed paralyse the present and may even blind us to the true value of what God is now doing.

ThE WorK Is StoppeD

It is an often repeated truism that where God is at work there Satan will be at work as well. This fourth chapter of Ezra calls attention to a striking instance of this very thing. The opening phrase introduces us to the adversaries, who opposed the people of the remnant and the work they were doing. The total scene might be used to illustrate the Lord's own view of His present purpose. He said to Peter and the other apostles, "I will build my church; and the gates of hell shall not prevail against it." (Matt. 16:18) In our last chapter the emphasis was upon the building, but now in this chapter we are to witness the gates of hell making a determined attempt to prevail against it.

So persistent was the onslaught itself, and so varied the tactics employed, for a time the enemy seemed to be having good success. Building work ceased and the entire project ground to a halt, until the second year of Darius. But then, as we shall see in chapter five, after fifteen years the work was resumed. And this resumption was brought about largely through the ministries of the prophets Haggai and Zechariah. (See Ezra 4:4,5 and compare v.24 and Ezra 5:1.)

Help Refused

The first approach of the enemy was very subtle, it was an offer of help. They would co-operate with the remnant in the building of the Temple of the Lord. Zerubbabel's reply is a model for us all. He said, "You have nothing to do with us to build a house unto our God." (v.3) Here is a principle of universal application. Before we can build for God, God Himself must be our God. Human reason might argue that an advantage gained from any source should be welcomed. And many sincere Christians have fallen into this error, and in the work of God have associated with themselves those who are not truly yielded to the Lord. This is an unwarranted charity and Zerubbabel would have none of it.

The wisdom of the builders and the aptness of the stand they took became immediately apparent. The adversaries were soon revealed for what they were. They began at once to molest the builders. They turned against them and terrorised them. They hired counsellors against them and did everything they could to frustrate their purpose. They even went so far as to send a mischievous and malicious letter to the king. The enemy had been clearly unmasked. He appeared at first as an angel of light but was very soon revealed as a roaring lion.

How very important are those many biographical sketches and personal insights God has given us of His people in His word. They show that, in principle, the experience of those who follow the Lord to-day, is no different from the experience of others in ages past. The histories of God's ways with men and women of faith are recorded for our learning. Those sacred records give us many wonderful and relevant patterns, and we do well to study them and to learn from them.

In every age the believer's supreme purpose is to stand perfect and complete in all the will of God. But the enemy will always contest that ground. Invariably he will do so with the same objective in view as of old and using the same modus operandi. However, every stratagem and device of Satan is exposed in advance by the scriptures of truth. This must be so, for in His word, God has given to us all things that pertain unto life and godliness. And as we learn to use that word aright so we are able to quench all the fiery darts of the wicked one.

Self-pity sometimes causes us to think that our case is exceptional, if not unique. But the word of God enables us to get things into perspective. It promotes within us a right attitude of heart and mind by showing us that no temptation has overtaken us but such as is common to man. It also assures us that God is faithful, and that He will not permit us to be tempted beyond what we are able to bear. Scripture also assures us that alongside the temptation God will provide a way of escape that we might be able to bear it. (1Cor.10:13)

The way of escape is not necessarily a way out. Most often it will be a way through. And so besides ministering to us the grace and patience we need to bear it, scripture will also show us that the circumstance itself is ministering to a divinely ordained end. Whatever the pressures of modern living, therefore, and however urgent the need for wisdom, the believer who makes God's word his guide will surely hear Him say, 'this is the way walk ye in it'.

Concerted Opposition

The conjunction 'then' occurs several times in this chapter and in the next. It suggests a sequence of thought and its repetition makes the sequence easy for us to follow. (See Ch.4:1,2; 4,5; 23,24 and Ch.5:1,2.) "When the adversaries heard...then they came..." The adversaries were the people of the land who opposed the people of Judah in their great enterprise.

When the ten tribes were dispossessed of the northern territory, the area had been colonized and these people were settled in it. The history tells of one occasion when God sent lions among them as a judgement for they were a wicked lot. (See 2Kings 17:24.) These people had been planted in the cities of Samaria and in all probability, had spilled over into Judaea by marrying Jewish women.

And so when God brought the people of Judah back to Jerusalem, the battle plan of the enemy was already laid. The great enemy of God and of His people always fishes with a long line. He had his agents already in place when Zerubbabel arrived. Years before they had been planted there by the king of Assyria and by the great and noble Asnappar. (v.2) & (v.10) They claimed to be 'worshippers', but Zerubbabel saw them as 'adversaries'. And now from within they acted like a fifth column, undermining the confidence of the builders.

Before leaving Babylon the hands of the remnant had been strengthened by all those whose spirit God had stirred, but now back in Zion, the people of the land weakened their hands. The enemy was at work, with withering and debilitating effect. We are told that they troubled the people of Judah in building. What they did is much stronger than the Authorised Version conveys. They troubled them in the sense that they actually terrorised them. They employed tactics that struck fear into the hearts of the builders. And they did this to such a degree that the entire enterprise was brought to an inglorious standstill.

Two kings are said to have reigned between Cyrus and Darius. The first was Ahasuerus. The term was a royal title meaning 'the venerable king'. His personal name was Cambyses. He was the son of Cyrus. The other was Artaxerxes. Again, a royal title which means 'the great king'. But he was an imposter for he impersonated Smerdis the brother of Cambyses and after only eight months he was slain. It was during his time that the order came for the work on the second temple to be stopped. (See footnote at end of chapter)

Letters to the King

The adversaries sent letters to them both, but the second letter only and its reply are recorded for us. The reference to the letters may have been the sacred historian's way of demonstrating that while the enemy is unrelenting in his opposition, the opposition itself and the strategies employed in it are never new. Both the offer to co-operate in the building and now the sending of letters to the king were simply two arrows from the same quiver. We have seen it all before!

Take for example, the second chapter of Genesis which records the completion of God's great work of creation, and then, in the chapter that immediately follows there is that working of Satan which resulted in the fall. Or again, take the case of Israel when their thirst had been miraculously slaked at Rephidim with water from the smitten rock, the next verse says, then came Amalek and fought against Israel. (Exodus 17) Ezra, in the chapter before us, selects an example from Jerusalem's history. And many more are the instances that could be adduced, for the pattern has been the same throughout all the ages.

The adversaries' second letter to the king proved immediately successful. It perpetrated a falsehood which, in the event, passed unnoticed. And so by default as it were, a cessation of the work was ordered. And that is how things remained for approximately fifteen years. The work did not resume again until the second year of the reign of Darius, king of Persia, commonly known as Darius the Great. And it was only because of the overruling providence of God that the halting of the work was not permanent. But once again Jerusalem had become a reproach in the eyes of all who passed by.

The letter was a very devious document. It made great play on the past sins of the people of Jerusalem. Our enemy is the accuser of the brethren and he still causes mischief by upcasting old sins. We must ever be alert to recognise such activity for what it is and also to recognise its source. But the letter also traded a lie. It said the people of the remnant were building the city of Jerusalem and its wall. They were doing no such thing. They were building the house of their God. The false report, however, sowed fear in the king's heart and moved him to order the work to cease.

It is a familiar tale. How often we have seen the work of God hindered by people operating from within. Joshua had to contend with the Gibeonites in his day, and Moses before him had to contend with the mixed multitude, and we have to contend with a great many who profess the Lord's name but whose loyalties seem to lie elsewhere. It is recorded of the adversaries of Zerubbabel's time that "They feared the Lord, and served their own gods." (2Kings 17:33) They were a people of double standards.

One of the most solemn references to the mixed multitude in the Christendom of to-day is from an apostle's pen, "Many walk, of whom I have told you often, and now tell you even weeping, that they are the enemies of the cross of Christ: Whose end is destruction, whose God is their appetite, and whose glory is in their shame, and who mind earthly things." (Phil.3:18,19) Such a statement should bring us up with a jolt and cause us to examine ourselves and to prove ourselves, that we are in the faith.

Opponents Success

The work ceased and the immediate cause was the opposition of the adversaries. But there was a secondary and even more pertinent cause. The deeper reason which lay behind what happened seems to have been a failure of faith. We shall see this brought out with emphasis in the next chapter, but in the meantime we can say, without being in any way judgemental, that Zerubbabel and Jeshua and those associated with them in the work ought not to have downed tools. He who had begun that good work would surely have brought it to a successful conclusion. Augustus Toplady put this beautifully when he wrote,

The work which His goodness began,
The arm of His strength will complete;
His promise is Yea and Amen,
And never was forfeited yet.

Resist the Devil and he will flee from you, and they should have resisted the enemy. They should have declared themselves on this occasion, as they did later, to be the servants of the God of heaven.

Faith is not always passive and negative, there are times when faith has to assert itself and take on an active and positive role. It was by faith the walls of Jericho fell down, and now a moment had come which presented an extraordinary opportunity for the remnant to assert that by faith the House of God would rise again.

Two Kinds of Faith

In all ages Abraham has been seen as the premier exemplar of faith. In his call to offer up Isaac on mount Moriah, we are able to see the two sides of faith. Isaac, allowing himself to be bound and laid on the altar shows a working of passive faith. This is the faith that waits patiently upon the Lord. Sometimes we need this kind of faith, but not always. On the other hand, Abraham, cleaving the wood and saddling the ass etc, manifests an active faith, the faith that gets up and goes. He had a clear and definite word from the Lord. He did not, therefore, need guidance, he already had it. What he needed was obedience and he was not found wanting.

The same things are seen at the Red Sea. The children of Israel were hemmed in on both sides by the mountains, while the sea lay before them. As Pharaoh and his hosts pressed upon them from behind they cried out in fear. Then the Lord gave Moses two words for the people. First, He said, "Stand still and see the salvation of the Lord." This required of them the passive faith of Isaac. After that He said, "Speak unto the children of Israel that they go forward." This called forth active faith: the faith of Abraham. And as they went forward the sea divided before them so that they passed over as on dry land.

Zerubbabel too, had a clear word from the Lord. And, as if that was not enough, he had the express authorisation of the king of Persia, whose word was law. The mighty Cyrus had issued a proclamation to which he had appended his signature. Moreover, Zerubbabel was acting in accordance with the words of both Jeremiah and Daniel, and everything was being done according to the law of Moses and after the ordinance of David, king of Israel. What then went wrong? The next chapter will supply the answer, but already it must be evident

that somehow faith had grown weak and the people of Judah were
no more "strong in the Lord and in the power of His might."

For Zerubbabel and his people this was obviously a time of very
great testing. The enemy had gained a significant advantage over
them. Zeal was flagging and the old enthusaism that had brought
them the long way from Babylon had all but disappeared. In such a
situation their instinct should have been to turn to the Lord in prayer,
but there is not even a suggestion of that. Happily, the story did not
end in permanent decline. God is faithful and He had not forgotten
them. In the fulness of time He began once more to move powerfully
in their midst and in the end the work was completed which His
mercy had begun.

O for a faith that will not shrink
Through pressed by many a foe,
That will not tremble on the brink
Of poverty or woe.

A faith that shines more bright andclear
When tempests rage without,
That when in danger knows no fear,
In darkness feels no doubt.

(Footnote - The order of the Persian kings mentioned in chapter 4 v. 5-7 seems to
have been as follows.
Cyrus. ch.4:5. First mentioned ch.1:1. He signed the decree which sanctioned the
exiles return. His reign began 558 BC.
Ahasuerus. ch.4:6. Otherwise known in history as Cambyses, the son of Cyrus.
He reigned from 529 BC.
Artaxerxes. ch.4:7. He was an imposter claiming that he was brother of Cambyses.
He was slain after a reign of just eight months. It was he who, having received the
letter referred to in ch.4:7, stopped the building of the temple.
Darius. ch.4:5. Historically known as Darius Hystaspis and Darius the Great. He
began to reign in 521 BC. (See under PERSIA Concise Bible Dictionary pp 610-
611.)

STANDING AND WITHSTANDING

It is a remarkable fact that the greatest of the prophets exercised their ministries in what proved to be the darkest periods of Israel's history. Elijah, Jeremiah, Ezekiel and Daniel are all examples of this. The chapter before us tells of a very critical time in the experience of the returned remnant. The enemy had gained the ascendency and the people had become discouraged. It was then, just at that point, God raised up two outstanding prophets, Haggai and Zechariah. Their ministries combined to turn the tide of events until the whole situation was redeemed.

Prophetic Ministry

The Hebrew prophets drew a sharp distinction between the circumstances in which the people of Israel found themselves at any given point and the God who overrules the circumstances. The constant and emphatic insistence of all true prophetic ministry was that any given situation, and especially the present one, whatever it may be, must be viewed from above, from the divine side.

Since the purpose of God cannot fail, it followed that whatever failure there may have been in the people of the remnant, God could not abandon His own designs. And so in the second year of Darius, the king, God raised up this dual prophetic ministry among His people. In the sixth month of that year Haggai addressed the people, (Hag.1:1) and then Zechariah addressed them in the eight month. (Zech.1:1) The result of these prophetic utterances was that new and zealous exercises of heart began to manifest themselves on the part of the builders.

Viewed from the purely human standpoint, the people could present a strong case for desisting from the building of the temple. It was important, for instance, that they should obey the order of the king. But looked at from the divine standpoint there was no reason for the work to cease. It was this distinction that the two prophets focussed upon and their emphasis eventually enabled the people to return to a true perspective on their work.

To outward appearance things may have been depressing indeed, but with God all things are possible. These two great prophets did not acquiesce in the conditions they found nor in the despondency and indifference of the builders. On the contrary, they began by addressing the root causes that lay behind the apparent causes.

It is a very interesting aside that the prophets did not content themselves with admonishments, however pertinent, they threw off their coats, rolled up their sleeves and gave their practical support to the builders. We are told that, "with them (i.e. with the builders) were the prophets of God helping them."

Haggai the Prophet

To appreciate the skilful way in which they analysed and responded to the situation, it is helpful and even necessary at this point to reflect upon their ministry, especially the ministry of Haggai.

The book of Haggai is made up of several carefully dated messages. After delivering his first message the prophet had the joy of witnessing a most encouraging response. "Then rose up Zerubbabel and Jeshua and began to build the house of God at Jerusalem."

The First Message

Haggai' first message pulled away the facade and showed that the pretext for inaction was only an excuse, and a very poor one at that. "The people say, the time is not come, the time that the Lord's house should be built." (Hag.1:2) We can always justify our failure to serve God by arguing that the time is not right. When the right time comes, then all will be different! But, somehow, the right time never seems to come. This intolerable attitude of mind, which paralysed the workers and hindered the work, was roundly challenged by the prophet. He chided them, "Is it time for you to dwell in your panelled houses, and this house lie waste?"

Excuses may have helped salve a lax conscience and explain an indulgent attitude but the real reason for their indifference had to be faced. They were more interested in their own houses than they were in the Lord's house. They were putting personal interests above every thought of God and of His work. In a word, they had abandoned the universal principle of scripture, so clearly stated by our Lord in the sermon on the mount, "Seek first the kingdom of God, and His righteousness, and all these things shall be added unto you." (Matt.6:33)

They might side step the issue by blaming the authorities for not maintaining their rights, or the adversaries for their lack of goodwill, but the true reason for their inactivity lay hidden in their own hearts. The Lord had lost His place and as a consequence anything relating to His name and work ceased to have priority with them. "Consider your ways" was the prophet's twice repeated challenge to Zerubbabel and his people.

He first confronted them with something of a negative character. He asked them to consider what fulfilment they were finding by their pursuit of the materialistic spirit. "You have sown much, and bring in little; you eat, but you don't have enough; you drink, but you are not satisfied; you clothe yourselves, but none is warm; you earn wages to put into a bag with holes." (Hag.1:6) His imagery was vivid, it graphically laid open their own secret misgivings. The prophet's word proved to be an arrow in a sure place. Let no one say that the scriptures are out of date for it would be hard to find words capable of expressing with greater accuracy the moral and spiritual condition of the Christian church throughout the western world today.

The Second Message

But the second message was a positive one. "Go to the mountain, and bring wood, and build the house; and I will take pleasure in it, and I will be glorified, says the Lord." (Hag.1:8) The verbs used in this statement should be noted. Go...Bring...Build. It is not difficult to find a New Testament parallel to these words. The Lord's great missionary commission still stands, "Go into all the world and preach the gospel to every creature." Our supreme task is to glorify God by bringing our generation to Christ.

Happily, these powerful appeals did not fall upon deaf ears. "Then Zerubbabel and Joshua, and all the remnant of the people, obeyed the voice of the Lord their God, and the words of Haggai the prophet." This is what the work required if it was to be resumed. It needed workers whose hearts were submissive to the word of the Lord. A nodding agreement would not do. There had to be a brokenness of spirit and a readiness to allow God's word through the prophet to become both their authority and their stimulus. They must demonstrate a heart response to the heavenly voice. They must become doers of the word and not hearers only.

The Third Message

In little more than three weeks Haggai was back once more. This time he identified himself to the people as the Lord's messenger in the Lord's message. The message for the builders was simple and direct and it must have brought them great encouragement, "I am with you, says the Lord." (Hag.1:13) Then, approximately one month later, he came yet again. His message this time predicted a glorious future for the temple it was now their privilege to be building. "The glory of this latter house shall be greater than of the former, says the Lord of hosts." (Hag.2:9) This may have anticipated the fact that the Son of God Himself would one day dignify that very house with His presence. (See John 2:13-22.)

Later still the prophet had two further messages. The first promised signal blessing upon the land while the final message seems to look forward to the establishment of the yet future millennial kingdom. Through the ministry of Haggai the Lord pledged blessing upon the people, glory for the temple and prosperity throughout the land. Those were heady days. Nothing could stand in the way of this great forward movement. Similarly, every true spiritual revival since that time has begun with a return to the word of the Lord and with our obedience to it.

Busybodies, Talebearers Etc.

But this did not tell the whole story. The second year of Darius, the king, was a significant year for another reason. Coming back to our chapter (Ezra 5) we read in the next verse "at the same time came Tatnai." (v.3) Immediately we suspect that the same old enemy is still at work. Of course the names now are different from those in the earlier chapters, the occasion is also different as are the tactics employed. The enemy is just the same but this time he manages to overreach himself.

In the instance before us the enemy presented himself before Jerusalem in the guise of a busybody. Tatnai was governor in Syria whereas Zerubbabel was governor in Judah. The former therefore, had no right to meddle in the latter's province. Some might argue that Tatnai was simply doing his job. And instead of listening to rumour he visited Jerusalem himself and then sent the results of his proper investigation to the king. But it is unlikely that Tatnai would have been uninformed of the authorising decree of Cyrus and in any case if he was simply doing his duty it is somewhat improbable that he would have been rebuked as he was in the king's reply. (See v.6,7.)

Quite obviously he wanted to show himself to be somebody of importance, and he may also have thought that by simply threatening them he would scare the workers off from building. He and his associates came asking a series of questions, all of which were calculated to that end. What were they doing? And what authority did they have for doing it? He went further for v.4 may be read, "They also asked after this manner, What are the names of the men who make this building?" It is not difficult to detect an attempt to intimidate the people.

Tatnai is a remarkable example of the talebearer, whom Solomon charged with sowing strife. (Prov.26:20) His aim, plainly stated in his letter, was to inform on Zerubbabel and his helpers. (v.10) The aim was to stir up opposition. But the builders had such a sense of the Lord's presence with them and of His eye upon them, they refused to be moved.

They did what they should have done fifteen years earlier, they stood their ground and the enemy was powerless to cause the work to cease. (v.5) He might huff and puff and he might even send a letter to the mighty Darius. But the king's heart is in the hand of the Lord and He turns it according to His will. Moreover, He is able to make the wrath of man to praise Him, and that is precisely what He did on this occasion.

God's Overruling Providence

Many times in the spiritual realm the enemy has overreached himself. On a certain occasion the Pharisees and scribes spoke disdainfully of the Lord Jesus, they said, "This man receives sinners and eats with them." (Luke15:2) Of course, they said this in malice, but did they ever speak truer words? The truth of what they said has been published across the world as a testimony to the sinner's friend, the one whom they derided. And here at Jerusalem we have another example of this very thing. What the enemy did only served to renew the courage of Zerubbabel and his people so that they persevered in the work.

Tatnai and his people sent a letter to Darius, the king. They sent it in malice, but, however unintentionally, the letter testified both to the greatness of God and to the greatness of the work that was being done. It also witnessed to the business-like way in which the work was being done. They said, "This work goes on fast and prospers in their hands." (v.8) God's work must be done in God's way and we must always ensure that the manner in which we do that work, as well as the work itself, ministers to the glory of His name.

The letter repeated the questions they had asked and recorded the answers they had received. Zerubbabel and his people unashamedly identified both themselves and who it was they served. "We are the servants of the God of heaven and earth." (v.11) Moreover, they were workmen who were not ashamed of the work they were doing. They boldly acknowledged, "We build the house that was built many years ago, which a great king of Israel built and set up."

They frankly confessed that their recent history was caused by their own ungodliness. For seventy years the chastening hand of God had been upon them. But they also testified to the overruling providence of God on their behalf. In the first instance, it was God who had delivered them into the hand of Nebuchadnezzar, king of Babylon. And now that same God had moved Cyrus to make a decree, authorising both their return from Babylon, and the work in which they were so busily engaged.

They were careful to detail the extent of the decree of Cyrus: (i) the house was to be rebuilt and (ii) the vessels were to be restored. And from then until now, they said, the work has been in progress, and yet it is not finished. (v.16) The unfinished task of that day speaks to us in our day. The Lord's present purpose is the building of a spiritual house, the church, and that work is still unfinished. In stressing the finished work of Christ on the Cross we must not forget His present unfinished work: He said "I will build my church." (Matt.16:18) The church age has not yet run its course and the still unfinished task means that there is much work for us all to do.

We face a task unfinished,
That drives us to our knees,
A need that, undiminished,
Rebukes our slothful ease.

A GooD FinisH

Upon receipt of the letter it would seem that Darius acted with a sense of urgency. A search was made, presumably among the archives in Babylon but the decree was not there. Normally, if the documents were not found in the records office, the search would have been abandoned at that point, but God was at work, ordering all things after the counsel of His own will.

Eventually, the claims of the builders were established when the original decree by Cyrus was discovered in the royal palace at Achmetha which was the capital city of Media. Then a reply was sent that put the Syrian governor, and his people, in their place. They were told, in effect, to get offside and to mind their own business. The king commanded them, "Be you far from there, and let this house of God alone." (vv.6,7) And so Zerubbabel and his people were vindicated.

God is Sovereign

What amazing testimonies we have in these chapters to the overruling of God in the behalf of His people. We have already seen how it was of God that they were delivered into the hand of Nebuchadnezzar, and then, in God's time, restored again to their own land by the king's decree. Now He overrules in the matter of the letter from the governor of Syria. Divine providence had preserved the original decree and that same providence guided the searchers to the place where it was found. In the end of the chapter we find the people rejoicing because their God had even turned the heart of the king of Assyria unto them, to strengthen their hands in the work. (Ezra 6:22) The whole scene testifies to the unfailing sovereignty of God.

This is an aspect of God's glory that we are only able to see in retrospect. As we pass through one circumstance and another we are sometimes tempted to think that God has abandoned us. Such is our perplexity at times, we are even tempted to wonder if God knows what He is doing in all the apparently contradictory currents that enter into the ebb and flow of our lives. But then, with the objectivity of hindsight we are able to say, "We know that in all things God is at work for the good of them that love Him." (Rom.8:28 NIV.)

All their Need

Evidently Darius was much impressed by the legislation of his illustrious predecessor and by the decree that carried his signature. It spelt out provisions which in the authorised version seem to gather around four 'lets'.

Let the house be built. (v.3)
Let its foundations be laid.(v.3)
Let the vessels be restored.(v.5)
Let expenses be given. (v.4)

And here the wrath of man was made to praise the Lord in a very practical and significant way. What Cyrus had decreed about the house itself, the foundations and the vessels, was adequate but what about the expenses? It was at this point Darius could go one better than his predecessor. He now decreed that provision be given to the builders, not according to some predetermined and limited scale but according to their need. (v.9)

Moreover, this provision was to be applied to the maintenance of the ministry of the house as well as to the actual building of it. And we must ever remember that this God, the God of overruling providence, is our God. Paul could write, "My God shall supply all your need according to His riches in glory by Christ Jesus." (Phil.4:19)

Darius' supplementary ruling revolutionised the whole situation. It meant that instead of a threat hanging over the builder's heads, the tables were turned, for the king warned of the gravest consequences should anyone drag their feet in the implementation of his order or in any way attempt to hinder the work. And if anyone sought to alter the king's commandment or to destroy this house of God, his own house would be pulled down and the timbers from it used as a gallows for his own destruction. (v.11,12) (See also 1Cor.3:17.)

The king's final word was this, "Let it be done with haste" and since our King's business also requires haste there must be a note of exhortation for us in that final word. The king's reply surely suggests that Darius was a man who had some knowledge of God. The marvelleous ways in which God had revealed His grace and power to Nebuchadnezzar and an earlier Darius were well chronicled and this Darius must have pondered those writings and learned important lessons from them.

The Task Completed

The closing verses of chapter 6, besides bringing the first part of the book to a close, describe the completion of the building of the second temple at Jerusalem. Through the combined ministry of Haggai and Zechariah, the people, with renewed zeal, built and prospered. Haggai challenged the people and stirred them up to a fresh sense of commitment, and Zechariah, the prophet of glory, pointed them forward to the fulfilment of God's purposes and the ultimate setting up of the still future millennial kingdom. God's people still need to be stirred up to fill their hands with service for the Lord. And they still need to have set before them the glory that is yet to be.

The history of Zerubbabel and his people after their return to Jerusalem might be summarised as follows,

Chapter 3	The building Commenced
Chapter 4	The building Ceased
Chapter 5	The building Continued
Chapter 6	The building Completed

Approximately four years after the beginning of the ministry of Haggai and Zechariah the final stone was added and the work was finished. Significantly this was in the month Adar, which was the last month of the Jewish year. And just as the completion of the house brought that year to a close, so the completion of the church, of which that house was a foreview, will bring this dispensation to a close.

As the work drew to a close some things stood out and have been recorded for our instruction. First, we should note how the over-ruling providence of God was seen working on their behalf, so that even their enemies were made to be at peace with them. What Tatnai and his people had been compelled to do, they did speedily. (v.13) We should also note the close link between the builders and the ministry of the prophets. (v.14) The former represent the work of God and the latter the word of God. How important it is for us, upon whom the ends of the age have come, to keep these two things in balance.

And so they built, and they prospered, and they finished the work, and all was done according to the commandment of the God of Israel. On the human level the project was begun, continued and finished according to the commandment of the kings of Persia. (v.14) Onlookers might have attributed it all to Cyrus and Darius, but the builders knew they were serving a higher authority, they were accomplishing a higher purpose. Such is the perfection of our God who in our own day still 'treasures up His bright designs and works His soverign will.'

The Celebrations

The completion of the house was the occasion of very great rejoicing. In the month Adar they kept the feast of the dedication.

The feast of the Dedication appears to have been instituted by Moses when the Tabernacle, the first house of God was erected. (Num.7:84) There was also a great celebratory feast of dedication to mark the official opening of Solomon's temple. (2Chron.7:5-9) And now, once again there was a joyous feast of dedication to mark the opening of the rebuilt Temple (v.16) This feast seems to have been incorporated as a permanent feature of Jewish life. Many years later we read of Jesus walking in the Temple in Solomon's porch at the time of the dedication. (John 10:22,23) It may be, as many think, that by that time the observance of the feast had come to celebrate, more than anything else, the cleansing of the temple from the defilement caused by Antiochus Epiphanes.

Be that as it may, the thought connected with this feast in its original concept seems to have been the ever present need for adjustment. We are told that in Zerubbabel's day, when the temple was completed, that the keeping of the dedication was a time for setting things in order. They set the priests in their divisions, and the Levites in their courses, and they ensured that all the arrangements they made had the sanction of the book of Moses, which in his instance was probably the book of Leviticus, although the reference may be a more general reference to the pentateuch as a whole. (v.18)

It is not difficult for us to discern in all these things spiritual lessons for ourselves. If we really believe that the coming of the Lord and the close of this present dispensation is at hand, we should examine ourselves and resolve, in the energy of the Holy Spirit, to make every necessary adjustment to the will of God so that we shall not be ashamed at His coming.

The following month, which was the first month of their year, two other feasts were observed, these were the first two of the seven annual feasts prescribed by Moses in the law. (See Lev. 23.)

Passover, of course, was a memorial feast. In it there was an acknowledgement of the fact that they were a redeemed people. They were not their own, they had been bought with a price. Joshua, when he came into the land kept the passover and thus acknowledged that he and his people stood there on the basis of redemption. In keeping this feast the returned exiles reminded themselves and proclaimed to all that the basis of their blessings, and of all God's dealings with them in the past, and all that the future might hold, was the blood of the slain lamb.

Before they could keep the feast of Unleavened Bread, leaven had to be expurgated, not only from their persons, but also from their homes. And since leaven is consistently used in scripture as a picture of sin, it seems that the keeping of this feast indicated a commitment on the part of the people to a life of holiness, a life of separation from evil. (There are six kinds of leaven specified in the New Testament and all of them represent evil in one form or another.)

The Twelve Tribes

Before proceeding to the next chapter we might pause to note that a great sacrifice was offered at the dedication. Twelve he-goats were offered for a Sin Offering for all Israel. This offering corresponded to the total number of the tribes of Israel. (v.17) At that point only a tiny remnant was present at Jerusalem but they kept before them the larger view of the people of God.

Many years before there had been the great schism, the ten northern tribes, later carried away by the king of Assyria, had separated from the two southern tribes. And even the latter, after the captivity, were still fragmented for only a small number came back from Babylon with Zerubbabel. Nevertheless, the people of God are essentially one, hence the emphasis upon the precise number of the tribes and upon all Israel. (v.17)

In recent years no subject has been discussed with more fervour throughout Christendom than the question of unity. We have already conceded that there is a false ecumenism, but this must not be allowed to obscure the true ecumenism of scripture. Alas, it is to be feared that many have failed to grasp the very great importance the New Testament attaches to the oneness of God's people.

Ephesians chapter four is particularly pertinent to this, it presents the subject in a three-fold way

(i) A Spiritual Reality. Eph.4:3-6.
(ii) A Practical Goal. Eph.4:1-2.
(iii) An Ultimate Hope. Eph. 4:13.

Believers are One Body

We repeat our earlier assertion that by the baptism of the Spirit, on the day of Pentecost, individual believers were formed into one body and thus the mystical body of Christ was brought into being. To-day, believers are made partakers of the Spirit's baptism at conversion and thus they are incorporated into that mystical body, which is the Church.

In a day of alarming fragmentation, when every man does what is right in his own eyes, we cannot stress often enough that true believers are not simply a collection of individuals, they are members one of another because they are members together in the body of Christ. The union of husband and wife in the marriage covenant is the earthly parallel to this heavenly union between Christ and His people.

Our oneness in Christ is a bond that has been formed by the Spirit of God. It is our pressing duty to recognise this oneness and to nurture it in the bond of peace. We do this by guarding our manner of living. As we seek to walk worthy of our calling, the Holy Spirit produces in us those graces, such as humbleness and gentleness, which are so essential if strife and division are to be avoided. Even in the event of persistent provocation, the Holy Spirit can produce within the trusting heart a spirit of patience and tolerance that will enable us to "forbear with one another in love." (Eph.4:2)

We can only mourn the fact that a failure to understand the true nature of Christian unity has occasioned much unnecessary division among Christians, especially in the evangelical tradition. Some have confused unity with uniformity. But it is quite apparent, even in the most closely knit of human families, that uniformity is nowhere present nor is it always even a desirable goal.

Unity and Diversity

Nor must we confuse this unity with unanimity for in the pursuit of truth there has to be much exercise of heart and it is through the interchange of seemingly conflicting opinions that we come ultimately to understand and know the truth. There is a rich diversity in the evangelical tradition, and, if that is simply set aside in favour of some spurious unity, which is not 'the unity of the Spirit', we shall all be greatly impoverished.

But 'the unity of the Spirit' will only find its complete expression at the coming again of our Lord Jesus Christ. Only then will the church, now in Heaven, and the church still upon earth, be revealed as one church. Only then will we all come "in the unity of the faith, unto the perfect man, unto the measure of the stature of the fulness of Christ." (Eph.4:13)

In our passage, some might say that we have a foreshadowing of that coming day in the sacrifice for all Israel, at the completion of the rebuilt temple, a sacrifice of twelve he-goats, according to the number of the tribes. The close of that momentous year does seem to point us to the close of this present age and to the return of our only Lord and Saviour. (Ezra 6:17)

The dedication of the second temple was a pale shadow of the dedication of the first. Solomon's sacrifice was greater by far. The visible sign of the Lord's presence, the Glory Cloud, did not fill this house. The glowing prophecy of Zechariah had remained unfulfilled, "Sing and rejoice, O daughter of Zion, for, lo, I come, and I will dwell in the midst of thee, saith the Lord." (Zech.2:10) At best, the first advent could be described as being no more that a partial fulfilment of this promise. It will, however, be redeemed to the letter in a future temple when the Glory Cloud will be seen again. (See Ez. 43:1-3.)

Nevertheless the dedication of the second temple was a very significant milestone in the history of God's people. It signalled a new beginning, a fresh start. It was a time of recovery and restoration. God had visited His people and granted them a little reviving and they were very greatly encouraged.

PART TWO

THE RETURN UNDER EZRA*

TO BEAUTIFY THE HOUSE OF GOD

EZRA 7-10

Ezra chapter seven
EZRA - MAN OF STATURE *65*
Ezra chapter eight
THE AHAVA RIVER *76*
Ezra chapter nine
CONDITIONS IN JERUSALEM *85*
Ezra chapter ten
PUTTING THINGS RIGHT *92*

* This Ezra should not be confused with another Ezra, also a priest, who came back from Babylon with Zerubabbel. (Neh.12:1) One other Ezra is mentioned in scripture, but he was of the tribe of Judah and a descendant of Caleb. (1Chron.4:17) Ezra wrote the entire book that bears his name but he personally features in it only from chapter seven to the end. These chapters chronicle the return from Babylon of a second company of exiles under the wise and daring leadership of this great man. Their eventful return, like that of their predecessors, is full of instruction for us.

EZRA - A MAN OF STATURE

In reading the scriptures it is important to observe that events do not always follow in a strict order of sequence or chronology. At the beginning of this book we noted that seventy years elapsed between the end of IIChronicles and the beginning of the book of Ezra. Here we must point out that an extended period of about sixty years lies between the end of chapter six and the beginning of chapter seven.

The portentous events described in the book of Esther also lay between these two chapters. (The princes mentioned in this chapter are probably the same as those mentioned in Esther. See Ezra 7:28 and Esther 1:3.) There we are told how the wicked Haman plotted to destroy, the godly Mordecai, and, with him the entire Jewish race. But God's preserving hand was upon His people and the tables were unexpectedly turned with the result that Haman himself was publicly hanged on the very gallows he had prepared for Mordecai. The same

God who had wrought marvellously in Jerusalem was watching over His people wherever their lot was cast.

The evil scheming of Haman was just another manifestation of the trail of the serpent, a trail which can be traced right back to the garden of Eden. It was in evidence in Moses' day when, by royal decree, the male children born to the Hebrews, were cast into the Nile. A very similar command was given by Herod at the time of the birth of Christ. Needless to say, in both instances the living God overruled the rulings of men and the divine purpose stood and prevailed.

The first promise of a redeemer, given in Eden, triggered off a whole series of attempts by Satan to frustrate the purpose of God The aim was to break the messianic line and thus to pre-empt the appearing in time of the Saviour of the world. Sometimes those Satanic schemes came very near to succeeding but, in the end, nothing could thwart the will of God and when the fulness of the time was come God became manifest in the flesh of our Lord Jesus Christ.

The New Leader

Haman's scheme had failed and eventually another man, a man after the calibre of Zerubbabel and Mordecai, was raised up to lead the people of God. His name was Ezra. Zerubbabel had passed from the scene and it would seem that in process of time the moral and spiritual condition of the people had somehow waned. But God had been preparing the new leader in Babylon, and now Ezra and some fifteen hundred people with him, set out on the long and hadardzous journey to Jerusalem.

In the chapter before us we are given three snapshots of this Ezra, whose express purpose in going up to Jerusalem was to beautify the house of the Lord. Firstly, we have an intensely personal view of the man. Then we see him in an official capacity and finally he is brought before us in a very practical light.

Ezra - A Personal View

In contrast to Zerubbabel who was a prince, Ezra was a priest and a scribe. He had a good pedigree and could trace his lineage back through sixteen generations to Aaron the first high priest of Israel. He was also a descendant of men like Zadok and Phinehas. The former had stood loyal to Solomon, the true king of Israel, and had won the priesthood from Abiathar who had foolishly thrown in his lot with a usurper. (See1Kings1.) As for Phinehas, at a critical point in the wilderness wanderings, he had showed himself very jealous for the honour of God and the testimony of His people. (See Num.25:7,8.)

Ezra was a man, therefore, who knew a great deal about priestly service, and his very appearing at such a critical period in the history of God's people was full of challenge for them, and it has been an inspiration to every succeeding generation. Four words are translated serve in the New Testament, three of them simply mean to do someone a favour. They speak of service towards our fellows. The other word is about service towards God. Jesus used this word in the temptation in the wilderness when He said, "Thou shalt worship the Lord, thy God, and Him only shalt thou serve." (Matt.3:10)

Much is heard about service, we are told that we have been saved in order to serve. We hear of service in terms of doing something for young people, old people, sick people etc. and such good work is to be commended, but we must insist that priestly service is different. This is service that has God alone and His pleasure as its object. As believer-priests it is our privilege to draw near to God and to offer sacrifices, not of sheep and goats, but of praise and prayer, spiritual sacrifices with which God is well pleased.

Mary of Bethany has given us an illustration of this kind of service. Her alabaster box of precious ointment might well have been sold and the money given to the poor. At the time many advocated that very course but she excelled them all, for she poured out her costly ointment upon the Lord's own person. Such service finds its stimulus in a singlehearted desire to please the Lord.

A distinguishing feature between Israel in the Old Testament and the Church in the New is this, Israel had a priesthood, but the Church is a priesthood. At conversion believers are made "priests unto God." (Rev.1:6) We call this the priesthood of all believers. We are "a holy priesthood to offer up spiritual sacrifices acceptable to God by Jesus Christ." (1Pet.2:5) And we are also "a royal priesthood to show forth the praises of Him who has called us out of darkness into His marvellous light." (1Pet.2:9) Together these two statements emphasise both the Godward and the manward aspects of priesthood.

A new order of Scribes

But Ezra was also a scribe. He is introduced as "a ready scribe in the law of Moses." (v.6) Whatever the status scribes may have had in our Lord's day, (and they certainly had attained to some notoriety), it is clear that their office had degenerated with the passing of time. Originally, the scribes were what we might call secretaries to the kings, and then later, during the dispersion, their work was to copy the laws of the nation. But in Ezra's day the duty of a scribe was to transcribe the sacred scriptures and then to explain and expound them.

It would seem that a whole new order of scribes arose at this time in the history of the nation. The men of this new order, de facto, took the place of the prophets and exercised a vital ministry during the inter-testamental period, the period commonly referred to as the four hundred silent years. The scribes were not prophets and their work differed from that of the prophets. The word they spoke was not a new word from the Lord, instead, they took the word the Lord had already given and applied it to the ever changing conditions of their people. Probably, we are right to think of Ezra as standing at the head of this new order of scribes.

Ezra's great love for his work was reflected in his deep reverence for the scriptures. He saw the law of Moses as something "which the Lord God of Israel had given." And the very words he transcribed, he regarded as, "the words of the commandments of the Lord." (v.11)

A 'ready scribe' is a phrase that applies more to his mind than to his pen. It means that Ezra was expert in explaining and applying the scriptures in the uncertain circumstances of his time. How he must have made the Law of the Lord his delight, meditating therein day and night.

Reverence for God's Law

Ezra imparted this reverence for the scriptures to the people so that when he rose up to read from the book of the law they immediately stood to their feet and continued standing all the time he was reading. He read distinctly, and gave the sense, and caused them to understand the reading. (See Neh.8:5,8.) The secret of his success is plainly stated, it lay in the fact that Ezra had first prepared his own heart to seek the law of the Lord, and to do it, and to teach in Israel the statutes and ordinances. (v.11)

Here is a man whose life was surely governed by God's law, for true godliness can only take root in the heart that is given over to know and to do the will of God. Moreover, Ezra proved his doctrine in his own experience before he attempted to proclaim it to others. Like the Lord Jesus, He was a man "mighty in deed and word." (Luke 24:19) Ezra prepared his heart, first to do, and then to teach, the ordinances. A preacher's ministry can only be effective in so far as his teaching is exemplified in his life.

It is a fact of history that in every movement owned of God the scriptures have always been prominent. Indeed, this might be taken as a fair test of any work purporting to be of God. We have already seen the vital part played by the prophets Haggai and Zechariah, in the building of the second temple. Now in the days of Ezra the same principle is in operation. And, in the next book, we shall see it again in the rebuilding of the walls of Jerusalem under Nehemiah. Since God has "exalted His word even above His name" (Psa.138:2) we must be wary of those so called movings of the Spirit that give little place to the word of God.

The Good Hand of God

But Ezra was also a man of faith. In these chapters there are constantly recurring references to 'the good hand of his God'. Ezra went up from Babylon, according to the good hand of the Lord, his God, upon him. (v.6) Again, we read that "he came to Jerusalem according to the good hand of his God upon him." (v.9) That journey was memorable for many reasons, but chiefly because every step was taken in dependence upon the grace and power of God.

Later we shall discover that before he left Babylon he was offered an escort of soldiers by Artaxerxes the king. (This is not the same Artaxerxes who had stopped the building. Artaxerxes is a royal title like Pharaoh or Sultan. The more modern 'Shah' is said to be derived from it.) The way was long: the total journey took a full four months. They carried with them precious treasures and their route was infested with highwaymen. In addition, there were quite a number of women and children in the company. But Ezra declined the king's offer, for his confidence was in God alone to bring them through to their destination. In this he was strong in faith, and God honoured his faith in a quite exceptional way. (See cp.8:22.)

Evidently, Ezra had often spoken about the good hand of his God upon him, and he was concerned in case some action on his part, such as accepting a military escort, might seem to contradict his frequently expressed confidence in God. His actions had to be consistent with his words. It is just here that we so often fail. What we do, does not always square with what we say, and, of course our actions are sure to speak louder than our words.

We, too, are engaged in a pilgrimage which will bring us ultimately to the heavenly Jerusalem. Ezra and his people are examples to us of how we are to walk and to please God. Their historic journey to the earthly Jerusalem is an illustration of what Paul meant when he said, "We walk by faith and not by sight". (2Cor.5:7) To say that we have 'faith in God' is not an outmoded cliche, it is the daily confession of every spiritually minded believer in the Lord Jesus Christ. The same hand that was upon Ezra for good, will still guide and protect those who trust in the Lord with all their hearts.

Ezra - An Official View

The amazing liberality of the Persian kings to Zerubabbel at the beginning, and now to Ezra may foreshadow the kings of the earth bringing their glory and honour into the New Jerusalem during the still future millennial kingdom. (Rev.21:24) Cyrus and Darius contributed generously to the return of the exiles under Zerubbabel, and to the building of the temple. And in the chapter before us we have a copy of the letter that Artaxerxes gave to Ezra authorising him to do all that the Lord had put into his heart. The letter was notable in that it made all the expense involved chargeable to the king's treasure house. Quite clearly this king looked upon Ezra as a man worthy of trust.

The letter was a legal document for it contained the king's decree and it also carried its own sanction should anyone dare to disobey it. And yet there is in it a remarkable blend of grace and truth. This is seen in the opening sentences. There are many references to the principle of the willing mind. The emphasis, again and again, is upon the voluntary and freewill nature of the work.

The letter stated that all Israelites, priests and Levites throughout the whole realm who were minded to do so, of their own freewill, could accompany Ezra to Jerusalem. They would carry with them silver and gold which the king and his counsellors had freely offered to the God of Israel. And, in addition, their charge would include all the freewill offerings of the people and of the priests, who offered willingly for the house of their God at Jerusalem. (v.13-17)

The psalmist David envisaged God's people being willing in the day of His power. (See Psa.110:3.) Although this reference looks forward to a time that is even now still future, it expresses a condition of soul we should always strive to maintain. This same willingness was seen in an earlier day, when Moses was making the tabernacle in the wilderness. All the materials needed were supplied by the freewill offerings of the people. The giving was not left to a few, for everyone had a contribution to make. But neither coercion nor compulsion of any kind were used, the giving was entirely voluntary. Above all, the offerings were given lovingly. "Of every man that gives it willing with his heart you shall take my offering." (Ex.25:2)

And here we are able to see the same principle operating in Ezra's day, and it would be happy for the church if that principle governed all believers to-day. On one occasion, Paul, confronted by urgent need turned to the Corinthians for help, and in his appeal he used the churches of Macedonia as an example. (See 2Cor.8.) "This they did, not as we had hoped, but first gave themselves to the Lord, and then to us by the will of God." God still takes pleasure in the gifts of those who have first given themselves to Him. The pressing need is not so much for consecrated gifts, but for consecrated givers.

A fair measurement of the working of divine grace in our lives is the extent to which we can say, "Not my will, but thine be done." For the willing mind so much in evidence in Ezra's day, was harnessed and subjected to the ultimate will of God. (v.18) Willing in the day of His power! So it was among that second company of exiles who returned from Babylon, and that very willingness constitutes an enormous challenge to us in our careless ease. "If there be first a ready mind" said Paul, and there is no substitute for such a condition among believers.

Oh for the floods on a thirsty land,
Oh for a mighty revival;
Oh for a sanctified fearless band,
Ready to hail its arrival.

There are a number of telling phrases used throughout the king's letter which we could reflect upon with profit. For instance, the king decreed that the treasurers beyond the river should give to Ezra whatever he required including salt without prescribing how much.

We usually speak of a pinch, a packet or a pound of salt but, interestingly, salt is never specified by amount in scripture. The primary purpose of salt is to preserve from corruption and so it might speak to us of the gracious words of Christ, which will keep us from sin, if we hide them in our hearts.

"Let your speech be always with grace, seasoned with salt." (Col.4:6) This was ever true of Him, of whom it was said, "They wondered at the gracious words that proceed-ed out of His mouth." (Luke4:22) Again, we are told that "Grace was poured into His lips." (Psa.45:2) Like the king's salt the grace that was found in Christ was without measure. We read of 'the grace of our Lord Jesus Christ,' of 'the riches of His grace' and of 'the exceeding riches of His grace.' All these terms speak of grace without attempting to quantify it. It is 'grace which like the Lord the giver, never fails from age to age.'

Another telling phrase in the king's letter said, "Whatsoever is commanded by the God of heaven, let it be done diligently." (v.23) This is translated from a Persian word which means quickly or precisely. The advice given by the king is pertinent to all who name the name of Christ. King Saul of Israel was told that to obey is better than sacrifice and to hearken than the fat of rams. And our Saviour, in His final address to His own said, "You are my friends, if you do whatever I command you". (John 15:14) The very essence of Biblical obedience is enshrined in the first commandment. "You shall have no other gods before me." (Ex.20:2) The priority we give to the Lord and His word is always the measure of our obedience.

Ezra - A Practical View

The king's letter had been written in the Chaldean tongue. But now the language changes back to the Hebrew and Ezra breaks forth in a grand doxology, "Blessed be the Lord God of our fathers, who has put such a thing as this in the king's heart, to beautify the house of the Lord which is in Jerusalem." Zerubbabel and his people had gone up from Babylon to build the house of God but those who came with Ezra had come expressly to beautify the house. (v.27)

Whatever this may have involved, its spiritual significance must not be missed. We are exhorted to "Worship the Lord in the beauty of holiness." (Psa.96:9) Our house of God to-day, is not a material edifice, built of bricks and timber, it is a spiritual house. It follows therefore, that we do not beautify the house of God by erecting huge and ornate buildings. Since the Most High does not dwell in temples made with hands it must be wholly wrong for us to go to excess in the provision of imposing structures and with them, as usually happens, to abandon simplicity of worship.

In this gospel age living stones are being quarried out of the great quarries of humanity, and are being built upon the Living Stone which is Christ Himself. This is how the church universal is being progressed. And this church, this mystical body of Christ is, in turn, expressed locally in local churches or fellowships of believers. We are only able to adorn the church to which we belong by heeding the exhortation already referred to, and by walking in practical holiness from day to day.

Holiness is the normal law of the spiritual world. "As He who has called you is holy, so be ye holy in all manner of living, because it is written, Be ye holy; for I am holy." (1Pet.1:15,16) The term simply means 'likeness to the holy one'. From the beginning we have been predestined to be conformed to the image of God's Son. And it is by Christlike lives that we shall beautify our house of God.

A Man of Prayer

The chapter closes with Ezra's prayer of thanksgiving, he says, "Blessed be the Lord God". And what a wonderful God is the Lord. He is the God of our fathers.(v.27) This phrase probably takes in at least a thousand years of history, for in the beginning of this chapter we noted how Ezra traced his lineage back through sixteen generations to Aaron, the first high priest of Israel. And now as the chapter closes we hear him blessing the Lord God of his fathers.

But God is not only throughout all history, He is also above all authority. For it was He who had put it into the king's heart to do such a thing. Artaxerxes was not a tin-pot dictator. He was the unchallenged head of the superpower of that time. His word was law, and the law of the Medes and Persians did not change. But an ancient proverb says, "The king's heart is in the hand of the Lord, like the rivers of water; He turns it whithersoever He will. (Prov.21:1) It was the Lord who had put all these things into the king's heart.

Ezra freely confesses, that for God to have extended mercy to him personally in the presence of the king, and his counsellors, and before all the king's mighty princes, was the greatest wonder of all. (v.27,28) Ezra was bowed low in worship as he considered both the transcendence and the immanence of God. These same two things, apparently contradictory, had exercised the mind of Isaiah, an earlier prophet, and moved him to write, "Thus saith the high and lofty One who inhabiteth eternity, whosename is Holy: I dwell in the high and holy place, with him also who is of a contrite and humble spirit, to revive the spirit of the humble, and to revive the heart of the contrite ones" (Isa. 56:15).

We can assert with confidence that our God is all that He claims to be, and this was marvellously demonstrated in the experience of Ezra. Reflecting on these things, Ezra's final word was this, "I was strengthened as the hand of the Lord, my God, was upon me. And I gathered together out of Israel chief men to go up with me."

THE AHAVA RIVER

This chapter is very similar to chapter two, and both are like pages from the book of life. The chapter lists the names of the males who came back to Zion with Ezra. It is a quite common practice in scripture to classify people under the names of the heads of their families. The absence of any reference to women has prompted some to conclude that this was the cause of the mixed marriages referred to in the next chapter. But since 'little ones' are mentioned it might be more reasonable to assume that women were also included in the number.

The total company amounted to between fifteen hundred and two thousand. This was quite a small number in view of the King's benevolent decree and his open-handed generosity. Two things may have accounted for this; the majority of the people had probably put their roots down so deeply in Babylon, they could not bring themselves to break the ties that held them. On the other hand, history may simply have been repeating itself for in every age those who remain true to the Lord are usually just a tiny remnant.

The People Reviewed

Before setting out on his long journey Ezra held a grand review of the people. This was done close to the river that runs to Ahava, probably a tributary of the Euphrates. The story of this chapter is closely linked with that river. Entries in Ezra's journal read, "I gathered them together to the river that runs to Ahava." (v.15) And again, "Then I proclaimed a fast there, at the river of Ahava." (v.21) And finally, "Then we departed from the river of Ahava on the twelfth day of the first month, to go to Jerusalem." (v.31)

Ahava means a continual flow and perhaps we could think of it in terms of the Holy Spirit. Jesus said, "If any man thirst, let him come unto me, and drink. He that believes on me, as the scripture has said, out of his heart shall flow rivers of living water. But this said He of the Spirit, whom they that believe on Him should receive." (John 7:37-39) Spiritually speaking, there is a great difference between enjoying the fulness of the Spirit, which seems to be what the flowing Ahava represents, and living by a stagnant pool, which appears to be the experience of many believers.

The entire company spent a total of twelve days by the river. But the grand review took place after three days had passed. (v.15) It is quite striking how often scripture notices a 'three day' cycle. When Pharaoh suggested to Moses that the people of Israel could worship God in the land of Egypt, Moses said, "we will go three days' journey into the wilderness." Forty years later and before the people crossed over the Jordan into Canaan there was a further waiting period which lasted precisely three days. The passover lamb was kept from the tenth day until the fourteenth day, a full three days, and then it was slain.

We find the same thing many times in the New Testament. Jesus said, "Destroy this temple, and in three days I will raise it up." (John 2:19) And again, "As Jonah was three days and three nights in the whale's belly, so shall the Son of Man be three days and three nights in the heart of the earth." (Matt.12:40) Evidently, the three days is intended to remind us of the cross, and especially of the great truth of our Lord's resurrection and of our identification with Him. In practical terms it reminds us of our need to "Reckon ourselves to be dead indeed unto sin, but alive unto God through our Lord Jesus Christ." (Rom.6:11)

The three day period declares that being on resurrection ground, the life we now live is different from the life we once lived. For Moses the three days meant separation from Egypt and for Paul the cross meant separation from the world. Paul boasted in the cross, saying, "But God forbid that I should glory, save in the cross of our Lord Jesus Christ, by whom the world is crucified unto me, and I unto the world." (Gal.6:14)

It is self-evident that we are slow to learn the meaning of our identification with Christ; and yet the first verse of the Psalter should be enough to teach us that the godly life is a life of separation from evil and of separation unto the Lord. "Blessed is the man who does not walk in the counsel of the ungodly, nor stand in the way of sinners, nor sit in the seat of the scornful." (Psa.1:1) The three days spent by the Ahava river serve to emphasise that a separated life is a necessary prerequisite to the enjoyment of the Spirit's fulness.

The Missing Levites

The exercises engaged in at that time suggest moral conditions that we should always endeavour to maintain as God's people. A dilligent and searching examination of themselves took place. This resulted in a serious deficiency being discovered and then, eventually, remedied as the people humbled themselves before the Lord. It was found that while there were a few priests among the number there were no Levites.

Levitical service had played an important part in the wilderness journey. Bearing the Tabernacle of witness and the Ark of testimony through the desert had been the responsibility of the three great families of the house of Levi. Later, king David had organised the

Levites into courses for the service of God. And now in this mighty undertaking led by Ezra, there was definite work for the Levites to do but, alas, they were not there to do it.

How this should be a rebuke to our slothful condition. What an honour it is to serve the living and true God. And yet, when there is work to be done we are so often absent, as the Levites were in Ezra's day. More might justifiably have been expected of them than of others, for to whom much is given of them much is required. But in spite of their privileged position, the Levites had apparently settled down in Babylon and were content to remain detached from what proved to be a singular moving of God in their midst.

Ezra must have been deeply exercised about this lack among his companions. He surely looked to the Lord, and he consulted with men of understanding. Only then did he act and the Lord honoured him. A number of Levites joined him as well as some of the Nethinims whom David had appointed to help the Levites in their work.

The rest of this chapter is occupied with the long and momentous journey from Babylon to Jerusalem. Three things appear to have dominated the thinking of Ezra and his people at that time.

(i) The journey they had to make;
(ii) The charge they had to keep;
(iii) The account they had to give;
when they finally arrived at Jerusalem.

The Journey

It should be noted that there was nothing casual about their approach to that journey. They first gave themselves to earnest prayer for guidance. They wanted to know God's way for that is always the best way. And so they sought of Him a right way for themselves, for their little ones, and for all their substance. (v.21)

In passing, we should note how important it is for Christian parents to realise that God's way for them is also His way for their offspring, that is, until the children are grown and have come to years of understanding. At that point they must have freedom to exercise themselves before God, and we must pray that through exercised spiritual senses, they will come to understand the mind of God for their own lives. Until then, wise parents will recognise that their spiritual exercise will also embrace their children. In addition, we should not lose sight of how the remnant recognised that God's way took account of their substance as well.

They also prayed that God might guard them. Highway-men lay in wait along the road and Ezra and his people would be prime targets for such brigands. Besides the security of their persons there was the immense wealth they carried. They had vessels of gold and of silver and other vessels just as precious as gold. We can understand the concern which prompted the king to offer them a military escort. But, as already noted, Ezra had said so much about the hand of his God upon him, he was ashamed to take up the king's offer. Such was the character of this remarkable man whom God had raised up to lead His people.

This was not a time for faint hearts, it was a time for faith to be displayed. What a testimony it would be to that heathen king and his royal court, if Ezra could bring this unlikely company through that treacherous desert and up to Jerusalem unharmed. On the other hand, the acceptance of an escort might, in the king's mind at least, have been a tacit admission of some doubt about God's power to bring them through. This did not mean, however, that they acted in a smug or conceited spirit. On the contrary, they gave themselves to earnest prayer, and they prayed specifically about the journey that lay ahead. "We fasted and besought our God for this and He was entreated by us." (v.23)

In the event, what happened was a remarkable honouring of faith. Their's was a perilous path but God brought them through unscathed. Their approach to and their arrival in the holy city resounded to the praises of their God whose good hand had been upon them all the way. What Ezra accomplished in that journey was on a par with those exploits of faith listed in the epistle to the Hebrews. (See Hebs.11.) What a marvellous pattern for us who, having been saved by faith, are now called to walk by faith. Having initially trusted the Lord to save us, let us now learn to trust Him for everything and at all times.

The Christian life is a pilgrimage. Pressing on to heaven we are all the while passing through hostile territory. "Our adversary, the Devil, like a roaring lion goes about, seeking whom he may devour." (1Pet.3:8) 'Strangers and pilgrims' is how the New Testament describes the believers of this age. Strangers because we do not belong here; our citizenship is in heaven. And, since we are strangers, it follows that we are in this world as pilgrims, we are here as those who are simply passing through. The order in which these terms are presented should be carefully considered for we can never be true pilgrims until we grasp our strangership here. The practical implications of this double designation need to be prayerfully thought through by each succeeding generation of God's people.

The Charge

The holy vessels carried by the remnant were for the House of God at Jerusalem. Every one of them pointed forward, and bore witness in some way, to the person and work of our Lord Jesus Christ. Bearing these vessels throughout that long journey was a very heavy responsibility. How dull our spiritual senses, if we cannot see in their charge some practical teaching for ourselves. Viewed in the light of the New Testament every detail of that remarkable journey seems to reflect some pertinent lesson for us.

The vessels were holy and they who bore them were required to be holy too. (See v.28.) The prophetic injunction is, "Be ye clean, that bear the vessels of the Lord." (Isa. 52:11) Significantly, no unclean hand touched the body of the Lord Jesus after He was risen from the dead. And we must look to ourselves and ensure that no uncleanness attaches to us as we endeavour to maintain the Lord's testimony while passing through this world. To take the Lord's name in vain means more than to simply allow some swear word to escape our lips. It is to link in our persons, some iniquity with that worthy name by which we have been called.

During the closing years of his life, Paul laid several charges upon Timothy, his son in the faith. Together they highlight some of the things that enter into a life of holiness.

1Tim.1:18,19. "This charge I commit unto you, son Timothy ... war a good warfare; holding faith, and a good conscience."

1Tim.5:21,22. "I charge you before God, and the Lord Jesus Christ, and the elect angels ... keep yourself pure."

1Tim.6:13,14. "I charge you in the sight of God ... keep this commandment without spot, unrebukeable, until the appearing of our Lord Jesus Christ."

Like Timothy, we too, are under authority. The testimony of Christ has been committed into our hands. We are in the position of the man in the parable to whom had been given a pound to be traded during the time of his master's absence. And then on his return, he was called to report what he had gained by trading. Our pound is the glorious gospel. We are to use the gospel to extend our Master's interests now and we are to do so as those who will give account before the judgement seat of Christ. The watchword is 'Faithfulness.' May we be faithful until the Lord shall come.

A charge to keep I have
A God to glorify.
A never dying soul to save
And fit it for the sky.

The Account

Upon their arrival at Jerusalem a further three day period was allowed to pass, and then, on the fourth day the weigh-in began.

They brought their charge to the House of God where all the vessels were recorded both by number and by weight. This solemn duty was undertaken by the Levites, who had as their overseer a priest named Meremoth. This Meremoth is also mentioned by Nehemiah as one of those who helped in building again the walls of Jerusalem.

We are informed that "We must all appear before the judgement seat of Christ, that each one may receive what is due to him for the things done while in the body, whether it be good or bad." (2Cor.5:10) Believers will not come into judgement respecting their sins, these were judged at Calvary and they shall not be remembered against us any more for ever. Judicially, the sin question was settled in the death of cross. But service will be reviewed at Christ's judgement seat.

This judgement, which should be distinguished from the great white throne judgement, is sometimes called a judgement of reward. Believers will be rewarded for their faithfulness, while unfaithfulness will suffer loss [ie. loss of reward]. The rewards have in view the millennial kingdom, for they will be exercised during that age when we shall reign with Christ. In some cases, there will be an abundant entrance into the kingdom, while in others, there will be a sense of shame and of loss.

The judgement seat of Christ should not be thought of as some kind of children's party where prizes may be distributed without discrimination. It will be a judgement in every sense of the term. The practical use we have made of our ransomed powers since conversion, will be passed under review in His presence, whose eyes are as a flame of fire. And the quality of every man's work will be tested.

True believers are building on the rock but the materials we are using will be put to the test in that day. They will either be purified by the fire, like gold, silver and precious stones, or they will be burned up like wood, hay and stubble. (See 1Cor.3:12-15.) It is the sort of service we render that is all important. Quality rather than quantity is all important in spiritual service. Works of greatness, as we thought them, may appear of little value. On the other hand, long forgotten deeds of kindness will have the Master's praise.

The old version reads, 'we must all appear before the judgement seat of Christ,' the word 'appear' means, that all will be manifested in that day. Things done in secret, known only to oneself and to God, will be brought to light. Every believer should keep in view the judgement seat of Christ. It will be a stringent examination of our service for the Master. It will also be an individual investigation for "each one of us shall give account of himself." (Rom.14:12.R.V.)

An additional and very practical lesson is also bound up with the careful weighing of the precious vessels at both ends of the journey. That whole undertaking had to be seen to be above suspicion. We are taught to abstain even from the appearance of evil. Paul laid down the principle which is to guide the New Testament church, he said "Provide for honest things, not only in the sight of the Lord, but also in the sight of men." (2Cor.8:21)

Jerusalem at Last

The last two chapters of this book describe the conditions the remnant found when they arrived at Jerusalem. They make very searching reading. It follows therefore, that the closing verse of our present chapter is really the last word about the remnant that came with Ezra. They fulfilled their mission. And then having first acknowledged the Lord in the offering of burnt offerings and sin offerings, they rendered to Caesar the things that were his. They delivered the king's commissions to the king's lieutenants.

Finally, a kind of memorial or epitaph is recorded by the pen of inspiration. We read "They furthered the house of God." (v.36) In this they are also a pattern for us. We know that God's purpose in the earth to-day is to build the church, which, in its local aspect, is our house of God. May it be true of the writer, and of the reader, when the day is over, that they had furthered the house of God.

CONDITIONS IN JERUSALEM

As already indicated the remaining chapters of this book are occupied with the conditions that obtained in Jerusalem at the time when Ezra and his people arrived. The chapters identify the problem that confronted them and show how Ezra reacted to it and how a solution was eventually found. It was a serious situation. It was an echo of the situation that confronted Joshua at the time of Israel's defeat at Ai. (Joshua 8) In a word, there was sin in the camp.

During the sixty years or so that had passed since the first exiles returned with Zerubbabel there had been a flagrant breach of the law of the Lord. A breach relating to such issues as marriage and separation. "The people of Israel, and the priests, and the Levites, had not separated themselves from the people of the lands." (v.1) This failure was immediately observable in their very comfortable lifestyle. They were fitting easily into their environment and they seemingly had no wish to be disturbed.

World Conformity

They were simply doing the things that other people were doing, and for no other reason, than that everybody else was doing them. Conformity to the world of their day was accepted as being quite legitimate. And their activities were not just harmless pastimes; they are described as the abominations of the Canaanites etc. But the matter did not stop there: through intermarriage they had mingled themselves with the people among whom they lived.

Had they learned anything from their history, they should have realised that this grievous situation had overtones which impinged upon the messianic line and carried serious implications for the birth of Messiah Himself. And then, as is so often the case, the problem had become compounded by the fact that the princes and rulers were openly seen to be the greatest offenders.

The parallels between them and us scarcely need to be underlined. It is true that some have carried their idea of separation to the point of isolation, but many seem to have abandoned any pretence at all of the separated life. True biblical separation is not isolation as is clearly seen in the life of our Lord. He was the truly separated man and yet He was the friend of sinners. Separation is like a coin with two sides. Negatively, there is separation from, and positively, separation to. The latter is highlighted in the words, "Let us go forth, therefore, unto Him outside the camp, bearing His reproach." (Hebs.13:13)

And therein lies the key to an understanding of this truth; for where there is real separation unto the Saviour's person, separation will follow from everything that would bring dishonour upon His name. This principle should guide us in our walk and in our manner of living, so that the things we do will always be regulated by the glory of the sacred name to which we have separated ourselves. The principle itself is intrinsic to scripture. On the first day of creation week, God divided the light from the darkness. And in a spiritual sense He has continued to do that ever since.

Young Christians need to learn this lesson well in the early stages of their spiritual experience. That is why no one should lightly assume leadership among God's people, for leaders guide the young by example as much as in any other way. Ezra found the leaders in Jerusalem not up to their responsibility or they would not have behaved as they did.

A Leader Distraught

Ezra's reaction to the prevailing circumstances is both an example and a rebuke to us all. He did not simply shrug his shoulders and deny any responsibility for what was happening. Nor did he adopt a casual, easygoing, attitude to a situation that clearly reflected on the honour of God and the authority of His word. He was possessed of righteous indignation and overwhelming sorrow and sat down in dumbfounded astonishment until the time of the evening sacrifice.

Ezra was first brought before us as a man who had prepared his heart to seek the law of the Lord, to do it, and to teach it in Israel. (See Ezra 7:10.) Upon his arrival in Jerusalem he must have called to mind the words of Moses, "When the Lord your God shall deliver them [those nations] before you, you shall smite them and utterly destroy them... neither shall you make marriages with them; your daughter you shall not give unto his son, nor his daughter shall you take unto your son." (Deut.7:2,3) The people already settled in Jerusalem when Ezra arrived in the city were quite clearly living in open rebellion against God and His word.

Backsliding has plagued the Lord's testimony throughout all generations. Here the people of Ezra's time had lapsed into the sins that had brought the judgement of God upon their fathers in earlier times. 'Old leaven' is any kind of evil from which we have been once delivered. If we parley with it we will surely become ensnared by it again. Even Abraham had to learn this bitter lesson when he succumbed to the very same temptation before Abimelech as he had earlier before Pharaoh, and that despite the earlier consequences. (See Gen.12:13 & 20:2.)

Ezra recorded the impact this situation had on him, and it was profound indeed. "When I heard this thing, I tore my garment and my mantle, and plucked off the hair of my head and of my beard, and sat down appalled...I sat appalled until the evening sacrifice." (Ezra 9:3,4) Ezra was no merely professional preacher, he was a man who felt in his spirit the burden and weight of the law of his God. He could not be at ease where the word of God was set aside and His worthy name dishonoured.

Those who Trembled

But God never leaves Himself without a witness. Those who had earlier come to Jerusalem were themselves just a tiny remnant. Now it appears that there was an even smaller remnant within that remnant. That smaller remnant is described as those "Who trembled at the words of the God of Israel." (v.4) Ezra became the catalyst that brought these trembling souls together, that they might publicly identify themselves on the side of truth. Quite obviously, the common bond between Ezra and this group was their common subjection to the will of God as revealed in the law of Moses. We might well ask ourselves, "where are the men and women to-day who tremble at the word of God?"

It is both striking and noteworthy that Ezra did not ask God to forgive His people. He simply fulfilled the conditions of forgiveness and left the issue with God. Sin in the life of the believer is scarcely considered serious at all in these days. But the reality is that such sin interrupts a believer's communion with his Lord and it also has an injurious effect upon his fellowship with others in the Christian community. And in addition to all that, it gives the 'accuser of the brethren' occasion to slander the offending believer before the throne of Heaven.

And yet there is forgiveness with God that He might be feared. But forgiveness does not come lightly. There are conditions to be fulfilled. An unbeliever, burdened with the burden of his sins must be pointed to the Saviour and urged to believe on His name for "To

Him give all the prophets witness, that through His name whosoever believes in Him shall receive remission of sins." (Acts 10:43) But when a believer sins he is urged to confess his sins that he might enjoy the forgiveness of God.

It is helpful to weigh these two terms which are quite distinct. It would be impossible for an unbeliever to confess the sins of, shall we say, forty years or of a lifetime. But a Christian must keep short accounts with God. At the close of each day he should pause to reflect and as one failure or another is brought before his mind by the Spirit of holiness, he should confess that failure before the Lord and seek His forgiveness. The precious promise to sinning saints who confess their sins is this "If we confess our sins, He is faithful and just to forgive us our sins, and to cleanse us from all unrighteousness." (1John 1:9)

There are two aspects to true confession. First, the sin that has been committed must be faced and acknowledged for what it is. We must call a spade a spade. And then we must turn from it; this is where repentance comes in. These two aspects of confession are seen in the final two chapters of this book. Firstly, Ezra acknowledges the sins of the people of Jerusalem. (Cp.9) And then he helps them to turn from those sins. (Cp.10)

The Evening Sacrifice

The fact that this intervention on Ezra's part began at the time of the evening sacrifice should not be overlooked. It is a timely reminder to us that sin in all its forms required the blood shedding of God's dear Son. The holy scriptures uncompromisingly assert that "Without the shedding of blood there is no remission." (Hebs.9:22) The atoning blood of Jesus is the only ground upon which God can forgive the sins of either the unsaved or the saved. We can rejoice that there is a sufficiency in that blood to meet the need of both and of all.

The true intercessor will always identify himself with those for whom he interceeds. This was certainly true of Ezra. Notice that he spoke, for the most part, in the first person plural. Falling upon his knees he cast his mind back to the beginning of the captivity and referred to our iniquities, our trespasses. He reflected on the long history of his people, it seemed one long and lamentable story of failure and sin. And then, he returned thanks to God that He had granted them grace for a little moment, and had given them a little reviving in their bondage. (v.8)

He acknowledged the innate weakness of their position and rejoiced in the mercy of God in giving them favour in the sight of the kings of Persia. It was only by the goodness of God that they had been strengthened to return and to set up the house of God and to repair the desolations of it in Jerusalem. "And now," casting himself upon the mercy of God he asks, "what shall we say, O our God, for we have forsaken your commandments?" (v.9)

He confessed the faithlessness of his people and pinpointed their sin and gave the precise law they had broken. Then he highlighted the mercy and faithfulness of God, who had punished them less than their iniquities deserved, and had given them the deliverance they now enjoyed. (v.12,13) But Judah had turned again to folly, and so Ezra concluded, "Behold we are before you in our trespasses; for we cannot stand before you because of this." (v.15)

What a pattern of intercession Ezra presents to us. He fully identified himself with the subjects of his prayers. He had a profound sense of the righteousness of God and an acute awareness of the sin of his people. And yet, as we have already noted, Ezra did not pray for forgiveness. When there is known evil among the people of God the spiritual mind will always judge it, rather than simply pray for forgiveness. We should certainly confess our sins but this should be done with a view to judging the evil that has arisen.

Ezra's prayer (Ezra 9) was like the prayer of Nehemiah (Neh. 9), and the prayer of Daniel (Dan. 9), and all three prayers have much to teach us about the ministry of intercession. These three prayers could be described as vicarious prayers. The next chapter will demonstrate that Ezra's vicarious repentance was reproduced in the people and a great reform was effected. The next chapter will also show that Ezra's God not only hears and answers prayer but that He answers in a way that is above all that we can ask or think.

PUTTING THINGS RIGHT

The life of faith is a life of conflict, it is a battle all the way. Well did Paul, the apostle, say, "Fight the good fight of faith." When Zerubbabel came to Jerusalem he found that the business of getting there was only a curtain-raiser compared to the many problems that confronted him upon his arrival. It was a similar story for Ezra. The latter was faced with issues of a most sensitive nature, issues that went to the foundations of family and community life. But they had to be dealt with if the blessing of God was to remain upon the great enterprise of faith to which he and his people had committed themselves.

Every movement of God has been accompanied by some form of reformation. This is the practical side of repentance and is always a necessary prerequisite to it on the part of God's people. Where the Spirit of God is moving in power, things have to be judged and many matters may have to be put right and because judgement must begin at the house of God, this can be, and often is, a painful business and it surely was so in the case before us.

Ezra, however, did not act in haste. He took time to wait upon God in prayer. (The change in this verse from the first to the third person does not denote a change of author. This practice is quite common in scripture.) And it soon became evident that what Ezra was about to do was of God. God was at work in the hearts of the people and before long "there gathered unto him a great congregation of men, women and children." (v.1) It was clear that these people were profoundly moved and that they were already conscious of the chastening hand of God upon them. We read that the people wept bitterly.

Godly Sorrow

The same sorrow of heart and the confessions expressed by Ezra in the previous chapter were now reproduced in the people. They came together and covenanted to bring their manner of living practically into line with the clear instruction that God had given them in the law. One of their number, Shechaniah, encouraged Ezra to be strong in his resolve to redeem the distressing situation that had arisen, he said "Arise for this matter belongs to you: we will be with you: be of good courage and do it." (v.4)

At this point it is important to keep in mind that Ezra, besides being the spiritual leader of the people, was invested with civil authority as well. This simple fact, if borne in mind, will help us find our way through what otherwise must be a very difficult chapter. The Law of Moses required the putting away of those wives and their children who were regarded as unclean and, therefore, not to be admitted into the assembly of Israel. For our part, we are not under Law but under Grace. And grace teaches us that within marriage an unbelieving partner is sanctified by a believing partner and their children are said to be holy. (See 1Cor.7.)

The New Testament normally represents the marriage bond as an indissoluble and life long union between a man and a woman who have been lawfully joined together. It does not therefore, advocate the putting away of partners to whom we are legally married; but this is the very thing that was asked of the people of Jerusalem. We are assuming, of course, that those marriages had been legally constituted.

If anyone should retort, "Then this chapter does not apply today!" we hasten to point out that the principles underlying the chapter are of abiding application. This is the wonderful thing about God's book. Times change, situations and circumstances change. And the issues facing the people of God may differ from one generation to another but God does not change and His word is pertinent to every generation.

There is no experience into which we might come but God's word will guide us and teach us what we should do. However sophisticated and advanced we may judge our modern society to be, the scripture still stands, "In all your ways acknowledge Him, and He shall direct your paths." (Prov.3:6) Throughout all the ages those moral principles which are at the foundation of God's throne have remained the same and they are no different today.

Decisive Action

Ezra and his people resolved to act along the following four lines;

1. Priority would be given to self-judgement. v.3.
2. Everything would be done according to the law. v.3.
3. There should be no undue delay. v.8,12-14.
4. Should any fail to judge themselves then they must be judged. v.8.

When the appointed day came a great multitude gathered to Jerusalem. The people were nervous because of the delicate nature of the matter in hand and, as if to compound the problem, the day turned out to be very wet. (v.9) And so it was decided that a commission should be established to handle the matter. This commission was set up under the supervision of Jonathan and Jahaziah assisted by two others. (v.15) Ezra was appointed chairman and certain heads of the fathers sat with him. They got down to their task on the first day of the tenth month and they completed it by the first day of the new year. (v.16,17)

The chapter closes with a long list of persons, some belonging to the priesthood, who had been found guilty of the trespass in question. The priests are mentioned first because theirs was the greater trespass. As we have said, greater privilege brings greater responsibility and theirs was the greater privilege by far. In several cases the issue was complicated by the fact that some had wives by whom they had children, so that what was done must have had severe and far reaching consequences. (v.18,19.44)

Wisdom from above

That such delicate matters should have been so successfully unravelled, demonstrates the wisdom given to Ezra and to those who sat with him, wisdom that was surely given from above. Perhaps the most startling thing of all is that whereas the whole business must have had the potential for widespread dissension, there is not even a hint of a single dissentient voice to what had been agreed.

Those who occupy positions of leadership in the Christian church to-day are often perplexed by the issues that confront them. More and more problems of a domestic nature are presenting themselves. Leaders must always keep before them the glory of God and endeavour to maintain the integrity of His testimony. At the same time godly men will seek the good of every member of the flock of Christ. And so they must judge every case that presents itself as those who shall give account to God.

The best judgement, of course, is always self judgement.   But where this is absent then the church must judge. The danger is that the church might act on the basis of some easy yardstick or maybe even on the basis of some cherished but untenable prejudice. In that event, untold harm can be done and needless reproach brought upon the Lord's name.

Ezra teaches us a vital principle in all matters of church discipline. Everything must be done according to the word of the Lord. This means that there must be a prior acknowledgement of the authority of scripture. "What saith the scripture' should settle every question. But then brethren must be in place who are able to bring the scriptures to bear on the particular issue that may have arisen. Such men are few and far between. There is a pressing need for men to arise who are giving themselves in private to the reading and the study of the word of God. Then when the occasion demands they will be able to step forward and show themselves workmen who can rightly divide and ably apply the word of truth.

Ezra also teaches us that in exercising discipline in the house of God, natural considerations must be set aside. What was done at Jerusalem certainly rose above the level of natural feeling or instinct. Too often matters are decided in the church, not on the basis of the issue in question, but on the basis of who is involved, or who might be offended, if a godly judgement is made. We must always be ready to maintain objective truth while remaining sensitive to the subjective consequences of every judgement made.

The correlative of this is that those charged with the exercise of discipline must be spiritually minded men. The spiritual mind is the mind of Christ. (1Cor.2:15,16) And the mind of Christ is the humble mind. (Phil.2:5-8) Herein lies the moral qualification that fits anyone to judge another. This was marvelleously seen in Ezra who, without any seeming reservation, commended himself to his people for this difficult and delicate task.

Identifying such men in the fellowships of today is not easy. But here again the scriptures come to our aid. When there is a breach among us, and this type of need arises, what are we to do? We should seek out men who will first judge themselves, and men whose supreme priority will be recovery and restoration. These will be men who are instructed in the scriptures, whose senses are sharpened by the Spirit of God and who have so walked with the Lord that they have imbibed the mind of Christ.

To the believers at Galatia the apostle wrote, "Brethren, if a man [any man] be overtaken in a fault [any fault], you who are spiritual restore such an one in the spirit of meekness, considering yourself lest you also be tempted." (Gal.6:1) The first principle in judging others is to judge ourselves. And the primary object in every judgement should be the restoration and recovery of the one who has erred.

It is not difficult to see why this book is called a book of recovery. It begins with recovery from Babylon, first under Zerubbabel, and later under Ezra. It describes the fifteen years of neglect in the work of building the temple in Zerubbabel's time and the recovery effected through the ministry of Haggai and Zechariah. And finally, it records the difficulties faced by Ezra and those who accompanied him, and the gracious recovery that God gave through the intercession of His servant.

And so the mighty enterprise to which Ezra had put his hand was completed. He had finished the course. But there was more work for him to do. About twelve years later we find him still in Jerusalem, when he stood upon a pulpit of wood to read the Law and to cause the people to understand the reading. The people's response was magnificant, first they wept, then they rejoiced and finally they observed the feast of Tabernacles. The record states that the gladness in Jerusalem at that time had not been witnessed since the time of Joshua the son of Nun.

ParT ThreE

ThE RETURN UNDER NEHEMIAH
To BuilD ThE CitY Of GoD

NEHEMIAH 1-13

INTRODUCTION *101*

Nehemiah chapter one
ZION'S CITY WALLS *103*

Nehemiah chapter two
NEHEMIAH COMES TO JERUSALEM *113*

Nehemiah chapter three
LET US ARISE AND BUILD *122*

Nehemiah chapter four
TROUBLESOME TIMES *129*

Nehemiah chapter five
STRIFE WITHIN THE GATES *136*

Nehemiah chapter six
THE TESTING OF NEHEMIAH *142*

Nehemiah chapter seven
ADMISSION TO ZION *149*

Nehemiah chapter eight
BRING THE BOOK *155*

Nehemiah chapter nine
THE FAULT LINE *163*

Nehemiah chapter ten
A SOLEMN LEAGUE AND COVENANT *170*

Nehemiah chapter eleven
EVERY MAN IN HIS PLACE *180*

Nehemiah chapter twelve
THE DEDICATION OF THE WALL *186*

Nehemiah chapter thirteen
NEHEMIAH RETURNS TO JERUSALEM *192*

INTRODUCTION

The book of Nehemiah has a similar backdrop to the book of Ezra, except that the Temple at Jerusalem had now been rebuilt and its various services restored. The period of the captivity had ended with the return from Babylon of Zerubbabel and Ezra and those who had come with them, and now, about twelve years later, this new book records the third and final stage of the recovery.

The events recorded here began in the ninth month (Chisleu) of the twentieth year of Artaxerxes the king. This is a very important marker because the much discussed 'seventy weeks' prophecy of Daniel, is dated from the time when Nehemiah received his commission to restore and to rebuild Jerusalem. (See Dan.9:25.)

The book of Nehemiah, as well as being largely autobiographical, records the closing history of the Old Testament period. The prophecy of Malachi, written just a few years later, also casts much needed light upon the spiritual condition of the people of God in Jerusalem at that time. We have seen in the book of Ezra that those who had earlier returned to Jerusalem came, first to build, and then to beautify the house of God. But the people who returned with Nehemiah came to restore the city of God.

A Significant Order

In all probability there is a moral order in the three sequential stages of the recovery. Building and beautifying the house suggests the thought of giving God His place, whereas repairing of the city's walls and gates suggests the idea of keeping the world in its place. When God established a place of blessing He always put an enclosure around it. A striking example of this was the Tabernacle in the wilderness. It is not any different to-day. There is an enemy at work, and because of that the gospel has to be defended and the testimony of Christ guarded. And so faith must still build its wall.

At any rate, these two concepts are simple and elementary principles of the Christian life. If we should fail to accord pre-eminence to the Lord Himself, then we shall invariably lapse into a kind of lifestyle which will not in any way adorn the doctrine of God our Saviour. The only effective safeguard against the encroachments of the world, is to give the Lord the throne of our hearts. Sanctify Christ as Lord in your hearts, said Peter, and when we do that, other things will find their due place.

This, then, is what the book before us is all about. Beyond the historical detail there is a spiritual education to be had in pondering these pages. In Nehemiah we have a man intent upon giving God the first place in his life. Whatever his attainment in the secular world, and it was considerable, the kingdom of God was always his priority. For the good of his people at Jerusalem, who at that time were suffering appalling reproach, he forsook Persia, and like a great forebear, he esteemed the reproach of Christ greater riches than anything the vast empire could afford.

ZION'S CITY WALLS

Nehemiah tells his own story with sincerity and charm. The book begins by giving us an insight into his status in the kingdom of Persia. He tells us, "I was in Shushan (Susa) the palace" (v.1) and again, "I was the king's cup-bearer." (v.11) To think of Nehemiah simply as a sort of butler to the king of Persia is to completely underestimate his station. Although he was a child of the captivity, like Daniel, he was skilful and wise, he was a man who had proved himself able to stand before the king. He had now become the king's confidant. In modern times we would say he was the king's first minister. And because of this he carried a heavy burden upon his shoulders. All the great affairs of the kingdom rested upon him. Nehemiah occupied a position of enormous trust and responsibility.

But an even greater trust weighed heavily upon him. Nehemiah had upon his heart the interests of the kingdom of the God of heaven, and to this, even the affairs of great Persia had to take second place. It happened that his brother, Hanani, and certain men of Judah crossed his path as they returned from Jerusalem. Having inquired of them concerning the Jews and concerning Jerusalem, Nehemiah was deeply disturbed by the quite factual, if somewhat graphic, report they brought him. The people were in great reproach, the walls of Jerusalem were broken down and the gates of the city were burned with fire. (v.3) Their report had a profound and distressing effect upon this great servant of God.

It seems that the reproach his Jerusalem brethren were suffering fell with crushing effect upon Nehemiah for the record states, he sat down and wept, and mourned certain days, and fasted, and prayed before the God of heaven (v. 4). Reading the prayer that followed we are satisfied that here we have the text of one of the most remarkable prayers of scripture. And we are not surprised that the living God took up this man and wrought mightily through him.

The name Nehemiah means, an encourager. And some time later when he came to Jerusalem, it was said of him "there is come a man to seek the welfare of the people of God." Unquestionably, the Lord had first place in this man's heart. He put the kingdom of God at the top of his agenda and he demonstrated this by promoting the well-being of his brethren and by being an encourager of them in their distress. Another had said, and Nehemiah must have echoed the words, "If I forget thee, O Jerusalem, let my right hand forget her cunning." (Psa.137:5)

The word of God and prayer are the two pillars upon which faith will always rest. In both Ezra and Nehemiah these two things are repeatedly emphasised. But if a difference is to be drawn between the two books we might say that in Ezra the the word of God is most prominent, whereas it is prayer in Nehemiah. Zerubbabel insisted upon everything being done "As it is written" (See Ezra ch.3) and Ezra was a ready scribe in the law of God. (See Ezra ch.7.) But Nehemiah was pre-eminently a man of prayer. His book records this in a dozen instances. Time and again his heart was lifted up to the God of heaven. With Nehemiah, prayer was a matter of disposition. It was a constant attitude of heart.

Before we consider his prayer in any detail we need to pause and think about the conditions that so profoundly moved Nehemiah. The wall of Jerusalem was broken down and the gates were burned with fire. Later, when he appeared sad in the presence of the king, Nehemiah cited these very things as the occasion of his crestfallen countenance. Jerusalem was the place where the Lord had chosen to put His name. It was God's earthly centre. The state of things in the holy city, therefore, was a reproach upon the very name of Jehovah.

The Wall - Separation

The city wall had the effect of keeping undesirable elements out of Jerusalem. It also had the effect of giving shelter and security to all who were within. In a word, it divided between those without and those within. Because of this we can reasonably think of it as standing for the principle of separation. In the beginning God divided the light from the darkness and He has continued to divide light from darkness ever since. Believers are not to be unequally yoked with unbelievers for the very simple reason that light can have no fellowship with darkness.

And yet, probably no doctrine of scripture has suffered so much in its application as the doctrine of separation. The tendency has been to dwell on the negative side and to see separation in terms of not doing certain things. The proof of this is the multiplication of separatist groups that have fragmented the evangelical scene. But the emphasis needs to be placed on the positive side. The negative might embrace a thousand and one things, depending upon the circumstances of a given case. But the positive is always single. What then is the positive aspect of this great truth?

Biblical separation is always separation unto Christ. "Let us go therefore unto Him, without the camp, bearing His reproach." (Hebs.13:13) We must always line ourselves up without reserve on the Lord's side for the nearer we get to Him, the clearer we shall see what we must be separate from. In His light we shall see light, and we shall know, almost instinctively, what it is we must refuse. It is tragic how this vital truth has been abused by some and made to divide the body of Christ. In the end, it is by our quiet walk with the Lord in the light of His word that we are identified as a truly separated people.

This is why the Bible is always relevant. It sets forth great and weighty principles and then calls for personal exercise on our part as to how those principles should be worked out in any given situation. Because of this there is no circumstance through which we are called to pass but the word of God will afford us the guidance we need. But when we reverse the order of these things and put the negative first, then we get into the maze of endless controversies.

The Gates - Service

The traders with their wares entered into the city through the gates and the traders from within carried their wares out through the gates. Much of the commercial life of old Jerusalem is conducted in the gates to this day, and so it was then. The judges too, and the elders, met together in the gates. The gates, therefore, may reasonably be connected with the thought of service. On a number of occasions Jesus spoke of service for God in terms of trading. (See Matt.25:16, Luke19:15.)

What am I doing for the Lord? That is the question raised by the gates. All who are, by the grace of God, in Christ, will one day go to be with Christ. But, in the meanwhile, we are here that we might be for Christ, filling our hands with service for Him. The parable of the talents makes clear that while all may not have the same capacity for service, there is, nevertheless, service for all to render.

Our service is usually the work that lies nearest to our hands. We should never lightly refuse to do something for the Lord, however unimportant it may at first appear. Not only will we find great joy in serving Him, but through that very service He will enlarge our opportunity and lead us on to something greater. Experience has taught that every little service rendered increases our capacity for more, until our very lives are spent in His service.

It may be that our present spiritual experience is reflected in the condition of Jerusalem in Nehemiah's day. Having denied the Lord His proper place in our hearts, separation has been treated with a certain amount of indifference. And instead of finding our joys in serving the Lord we have been working at the flesh pots of a world that can never satisfy. If that is so, may Nehemiah's exercise of heart be reproduced in us, for our God is the God of recovery. He is able to restore to us the years that the locusts have eaten and to renew in us the joy of His salvation.

A Man of Prayer

Nehemiah's grief manifested itself in the intensity of his praying. With great purpose of heart and a truly humble mind he came before the mercy-seat. The prayer recorded in chapter one may have been a single prayer offered on one specific occasion, or it may be a summary of Nehemiah's exercise of heart over a period of time until, eventually, those events took place which are described in the next chapter.

Whatever may have been the case in this instance, prayer itself is primarily viewed in scripture as an attitude of heart towards God. It is in this sense that we are exhorted to 'pray without ceasing.' We must be careful to maintain, at all times, a daily, even a moment by moment attitude of dependence upon God. But, having said that, prayer is also a specific and definite act. And that is probably how Nehemiah's prayer should be viewed.

There are many such 'acts' of prayer recorded in the sacred canon. (See Ezra 9, Daniel 9, John 17 etc.) All these prayers are recorded for our learning and can be looked upon as models after which we may, with profit, pattern our own praying. Nehemiah introduced his prayer with a preamble that impresses upon us the importance of taking time to wait upon God. "I sat down and wept, and mourned certain days, and fasted, and prayed before the God of heaven." (v.4) Such language forbids us, as a matter of habit, to rush into the presence of God, mutter a few sentences, and then rush away again. There is an intensity about prayer that demands time and patient waiting upon Him in the secret place.

John Hyde, an American missionary to India of about one hundred years ago, was often referred to as 'the apostle of prayer' and to his friends he was known as 'Praying Hyde'. Passing through England on one occasion, he called on Dr.J.Wilbur Chapman who, at the time, was engaged in one of the famous Chapman Alexander missions of those days. Dr. Chapman asked John Hyde to pray for him and afterwards he recorded what happened.

"He came to my room, turned the key in the door, dropped on his knees, waited five minutes without a single syllable coming from his lips. I could hear my own heart thumping and beating. I felt the hot tears running down my face. I knew I was with God. Then with upturned face, down which the tears were streaming, he said, "Oh God!" Then for five minutes at least, he was still again, and then when he knew he was talking with God his arm went round my shoulder and there came up from the depth of his heart such petitions for men as I had never heard before. I rose from my knees to know what real prayer was." (Praying Hyde by Francis McGaw, p.62,3.)

The praying of John Hyde was akin to that of Nehemiah. David, the sweet psalmist of Israel, also knew something of this. He doubly exhorts us to wait upon God. "Wait on the Lord; be of good courage, and He shall strengthen your heart. Wait, I say, on the Lord." (Psa.27:14) In an age when we are more busy than God intended us to be, we must heed these injunctions, and recover for our needy generation the faith that waits, and goes on waiting, upon God.

By its very nature prayer is such a spiritual exercise, we hesitate to introduce technical ideas into it. It seems almost irreverent to think of technique when we come to prayer. But we speak of technique only in the sense of order and pattern in prayer. When Paul urged upon Timothy the need for prayer he used four terms which, when taken together, summarise Nehemiah's praying. "I exhort therefore, that first of all, supplications, prayers (acts of worship when human needs are set aside in the contemplation of the majesty and mercy of God), intercessions, and giving of thanks, be made for all men." (1Tim.2:1) The parallels between Paul's exhortation and Nehemiah's example are clearly instructive.

Now if we can accept that Nehemiah's prayer is given in such detail because it is intended as a model for us to follow, then we can and must analyze it. Since it is one of several mighty 'acts' of prayer recorded in scripture, let us use the word **acts** as an acrostic and apply it to this prayer. We shall find a definite pattern from which we can derive much profit.

A is for **Adoration**

"I beseech thee, O Lord God of heaven, the great and awe-inspiring God." Quite plainly, Nehemiah understood the times in which he lived, for he addressed God, not as the God of Israel, but as the God of heaven. The glory had departed from the Temple in Jerusalem and had not returned. (Ez.11:22-24) One day the glory will return, and Israel's national honour will be restored, but in the meantime, earthly dominion has passed into Gentile hands. Nevertheless, there was an unshakeable throne in the heavens which still ruled over all.

Nehemiah then focused on a definite facet of God's character. He worshipped God for His faithfulness. He said, "God, who keeps covenant and mercy for them who love Him and observe His commandments." (v.5) The faithfulness of God simply means that He is faithful to His word. The Jews had an immediate reason to rejoice in this truth. God had strikingly fulfilled His word in the carrying away of the people into captivity. And now, in the fulness of time, He had given further proof of His faithfulness in their recent return from Babylon. (See Jer.25:12.)

Perhaps we have had remarkable evidences of God's mercy in our own circumstances. Maybe, like the Jerusalem Jews of Nehemiah's day, we have witnessed, in some singular way, His faithfulness to us. We should turn such experiences into fuel for the altar of prayer. And coming to the throne of grace, we should take with us words that will in some measure express the adoration of truly grateful hearts.

C is for **Confession**

The true intercessor always identifies himself with those for whom he makes intercession. He makes their failures and their sins his own. This Nehemiah did. Although there are no grounds for implying that Nehemiah was personally unfaithful, in fact, no flaw or failing is recorded against him personally, yet he humbly acknowledged and confessed the unfaithfulness of his people as though it was his own. He spoke of "the sins of the children of Israel, which we have sinned against you; both I and my father's house have sinned." (v.6)

The first principle in forgiveness is confession. "If we confess our sins, He is faithful and just to forgive us our sins, and to cleanse us from all unrighteousness." (1John 1:9) It is easy to discover faults in others, faults of which they might not even be aware. But we must learn to judge ourselves and to take the same humble position before God as Nehemiah. We must confess the unfaithfulness of our own hearts before Him.

Nehemiah did not make or seek excuses for the failures that burdened him. He said, "We have dealt very corruptly against thee, and have not kept the commandments, nor the statutes, nor the ordinances, which you commanded your servant, Moses." (v.7) National restoration required national repentance. And so without reserve or hesitation he openly acknowledged the sins of his people and humbly identified himself with them in their failings.

T is for **Thanksgiving**

Paul urges us, "In everything give thanks." (1Thess.5:18) The preposition here is vital. We may not be able to give thanks for everything; but whatever the circumstance we can still give thanks as Nehemiah did. He pleaded the promises of God. The promises of God are sure, and for our confidence God has underpinned them by raising Jesus from the dead. "For all the promises of God in Him are yea, and in Him Amen, unto the glory of God." (2Cor.1:20)

The integrity of God's word has been demonstrated throughout history in both negative and positive ways. On the one hand, loss always resulted from disobedience (v.8), while on the other, blessing always followed upon obedience (v.9). These people had certainly proved the former in their captivity and they had also known something of the latter in their recovery. Nehemiah's concern was that they might know God's restoring mercy in even greater measure.

Failure at this point makes perpetual beggars of us all before God's throne. "Where are the nine?" the Lord demanded to know, when ten lepers had been cleansed and only one returned to give thanks. There is no day so dreary and no night so dark, but the throne of God remains settled in heaven. Let that fact rejoice our hearts and move us to true thankfulness.

It is an interesting study to note the occasions chosen by our Lord to express His thanksgiving. For example, most of His mighty works had been done in Chorazin, Bethsaida and Capernaum but those were the very cities that had rejected Him. It was then, "At that time, Jesus answered and said, I thank thee, O Father, Lord of heaven and earth..." (Matt.11:20-27)

It is said to be characteristic of the last days that men will be unthankful. (2Tim.3:2) And counting their blessings is certainly not an exercise with which many trouble themselves nowadays. But those who name the name of Christ must be different. We should be like Jesus who even in the day of His rejection gave thanks that God was over all, blessed for evermore. We should be like Paul, giving thanks always. And this should be especially so when we come to the mercy seat and bow before the God of all grace in prayer.

S is for **Supplication** (v. 10 & 11)

It is only now, at the end of his prayer, that Nehemiah comes to petition. As he prayed he grounded his prayer in the fact of redemption. "These are your people whom you have redeemed." In this he reminds us of the mediation of Moses when Israel had so grievously sinned in the matter of the golden calf. Moses said, "Lord, why does your wrath wax hot against your people, whom you have brought forth out of the land of Egypt with great power, and with a mighty hand?" (See Ex.32:11-14.)

Redemption ground is the place to stand when we come before God in prayer. Our Lord Himself, when He entered into the heavenly sanctuary, stood upon this ground. It was by 'His own Blood' that He entered in. And because His present ministry of intercession is based upon the blood of redemption, we are able to identify ourselves with Him by faith within the veil, and by virtue of that same blood to make our prayer to God.

But then, Nehemiah also established his prayer in the desires that filled the hearts of his people. "Your servants, who desire to fear your name." If redemption ground has to do with our standing before God, then these spiritual desires have to do with our state, what we ought to be in ourselves. Jesus said, "Blessed are they which do hunger and thirst after righteousness: for they shall be filled." (Matt.5:6) Nehemiah could plead what the Lord, in another place, called 'an honest and good' heart. This is the subjective side of prayer but it is very important and it is certainly very searching.

True prayer calls for a prior examination of ourselves. "If I regard iniquity in my heart the Lord will not hear me." (Psa.66:18) On the other hand, "If our hearts condemn us not then have we confidence towards God." (1John3:21) The Lord looks upon the heart; He probes the springs that motivate us, and He hears and answers the prayer that springs from hearts that are truly seeking the glory of God. Finally, Nehemiah asked that his own way might be prepared before the king, and just how amazingly God heard and answered that petition is the subject of the chapters that follow.

NEHEMIAH COMES TO JERUSALEM

The events described in this chapter took place some four to five months after the offering up of Nehemiah's great prayer of the previous chapter. The date is quite specific: the month Nisan, in the twentieth year of Artaxerxes the king. As already noted, this is the date from which that notable prophecy of Daniel, known as the 'Seventy Weeks Prophecy' must be dated. (See Dan.9.) According to Daniel, the cutting off of Messiah would be four hundred and eighty three years from that date. Just how precisely that prophecy was fulfilled has been ably discussed elsewhere.

During this time, Nehemiah doubtless continued in prayer and patient waiting upon his God. At length, the burden upon his heart affected his countenance to a degree that the king could not fail to notice. In the courts of those ancient kings the entire atmosphere was one of suspicion. Any appearance of agitation or any change in the behaviour or bearing of someone who stood before the king, made that person immediately suspect. In that context such an eventuality carried overtones of a plot against the king's life.

The incident before us might even have been more than usually suspicious, because Nehemiah was the king's cupbearer and the occasion of his gloominess was Jerusalem, which was known with some contempt as the rebellious city. As for his concern for the people of Judah, in those days they had become a by-word among the nations.

And it would be quite wrong to think, as some have suggested, that Nehemiah's sadness was feigned and was simply a ploy to elicit the king's sympathy. This would be unworthy and, in any case, the context rules out such a thought, for when the king noticed his gloominess and questioned him about its cause, Nehemiah states quite openly, "Then I was very much afraid." (v 2)

Nehemiah's sorrow of heart was so deep it could not fail to be stamped upon his face. And, of course, there was a cause. When the king demanded to know what it was, Nehemiah, whose heart must have been deeply stirred within him, spoke the truth. "Why should not my countenance be sad, when the city, the place of my fathers' sepulchres, lies waste, and its gates are consumed with fire?" This prompted the king to ask a further question. "For what do you make request?"

So I Prayed . . .

At this point Nehemiah tells us, "So I prayed to the God of heaven." This was a spontaneous, arrow-like prayer. It seems quite clear that with Nehemiah, praying meant more than simply saying prayers. Prayer was for him an attitude of heart and mind. He was a man who cultivated the habit of constantly inclining his heart towards God. In that sense he 'prayed without ceasing.' And so, in that breathtaking instant, between the king's question and Nehemiah's answer, his heart was consciously lifted up in prayer to the God whose ear is always open to our cry.

"He who dwells in the secret place of the Most High shall abide under the shadow of the Almighty." (Psa.91:1) This precious truth was surely exemplified in Nehemiah's experience at that precise moment. The man who abides in the secret place can, at any moment, and in any circumstance, refer any issue to God for guidance. Nehemiah may even have been mindful of how the Lord had said, "Before they call I will answer; and while they are yet speaking, I will hear." (Isa.65:24)

His request, when he made it, was clear and to the point. "That you would send me to Judah, unto the city...that I might build it." (v 5) Nehemiah's answer demonstrated that while the great city of Sushan lay at his feet, his heart was with the people of God in Jerusalem. In this, he was like Moses, who renounced Egypt, choosing to suffer affliction with the people of God, rather than to enjoy the pleasures of sin for a season.

So far God had wonderfully answered prayer. But there was more to come. The king now asked a further question. "For how long will the journey be, and when will you return?" By this time Nehemiah's fear (v 2) had given way to faith (v 5) and at that point, the faith itself was further increased and he was emboldened to set the king a time (v 6).

Faith always grows with exercise and Nehemiah is now further strengthened to request letters from the king to the governors beyond the river. He asked that authority might be given for him to have unimpeded progress in his journey. And then, in the end, little faith became great faith, for he went further still and requested a letter unto Asaph, the keeper of the king's forest. He wanted materials for the building work he planned to do. The granting of this particular letter is an illustration of the scripture which says, "And my God shall supply all your need." (Phil.4:19)

Prayer, be it prayer as an attitude of heart or as a specific act of praying, links us with the overruling sovereignty of God. Nehemiah found it so, for he testified that "The king granted him his request, according to the good hand of his God upon him." (v 8) Thus Nehemiah gave God the glory. He believed that "The king's heart is in the hand of the Lord, and He turns it whithersoever He will." (Prov.21:1) Earlier, Joseph, in Egypt, proved the reality of this. He must often have wondered if God had forgotten. But when God's time came, Joseph was elevated to become next only to Pharaoh throughout all the land of Egypt.

In the passage before us Nehemiah is careful not to abuse his position. And he is careful not to force a single issue. He had committed the whole matter into the Lord's hands and he must leave it there. When the resolution came, five months later, it must have been in a manner, and in a measure, that was exceeding abundantly above all that Nehemiah could have asked or even thought. (See Eph.3:20.) The over-ruling Lord had moved the king to ask a series of questions and the same Lord had prompted Nehemiah in his replies.

Beyond the River

Beyond the river is an expression occuring more than once in this passage. The Euphrates was the river referred to and beyond it lay the land of Canaan and especially Jerusalem, the city where God had chosen to place His name. Nehemiah's heart was already there and all his cherished hopes and aspirations for the chosen people, his own people, lay there. Babylon was a strange land and a true citizen of Zion could not be at home there.

Canaan is not heaven, for Nehemiah, like Joshua in an earlier time, found Canaan a place of intense and bitter conflict. But it does speak of 'The Heavenly Places', the sphere of the believer's present association with Christ. (See Eph.1:3.) We are already blessed with all spiritual blessings in heavenly places in Christ. And while we are not yet in heaven, we can be there by faith, and to be there is to enjoy daily communion with Christ. This is what is means to be seated with Christ in heavenly places. But to be there also involves conflict. "For we wrestle not against flesh and blood, but against principalities and powers...in heavenly places." (See Eph.6:10-20.)

The experience of Nehemiah in Jerusalem seems to illustrate the many and various dimensions that make up the believer's experience to-day who lives in the realm of the heavenly places. The rest of the present chapter describes Nehemiah's actual arrival in Jerusalem, what he did when he got there, and the plan of action he disclosed to his people.

Nehemiah's arrival (v.9 - 11)

It is interesting to note that Nehemiah came to Jerusalem accompanied by an escort of soldiers. Earlier, when Ezra had made the same journey he refused a similar escort. It may be that the reason for this difference lay in the simple fact that Ezra's mission concerned the temple, whereas Nehemiah's mission was concerned with the city. And the help of the secular power may, therefore, have been appropriate in one case but not in the other.

Or it may have been the case that in neither instance was it felt that any principle was involved, and so each man made his own decision. That their conclusions were at variance, might teach us that should such matters arise in the church, liberty must be extended by both sides of the argument to accomodate differences of opinion should such be expressed. The rule is that where spiritual principle is involved believers need to be of the same mind in the Lord. But when it is only a matter of procedure or of preference there is room for the freedom of every man's conscience.

An Enemy within the Gates

When he came to Jerusalem, Nehemiah found the enemy was there ahead of him. In this respect, his experience was no different from that of both Zerubbabel and Ezra. As soon as each of them moved to fulfil the will of God they encountered opposition, and in every case it was both intense and persistent. In Nehemiah's case Sanballat the Horonite, (Horon was a city of Moab) and Tobiah the Ammonite, were grieved at his arrival. They knew he had come, specifically, to seek the welfare of the people of God, and it was this that made their opposition so implacable.

The Moabites and the Ammonites were Israel's traditional enemies. They had a blood relationship with Israel but at every turn they opposed the people of God. They did not meet Israel with bread and water when they came forth from Egypt. Then they hired Baalim to curse Israel. But the curse of God rested upon them and they were excluded forever from entering the congregation. They answer to present day church members who are still unregenerate. A people whose profession is a pretence and whose presence in the church is a source of constant weakness.

We shall meet the representatives of these people several times in this book. But we should note that an enemy is at work in our day as well. In fact, the enemy is always at work, and if we are in any measure faithful in the service of God we must be careful to "Put on the whole armour of God," and to be always ready for spiritual conflict.

Three Meaningful Days

It is also noteworthy that Nehemiah, after he came to Jerusalem, allowed three days to elapse before making any definite move. This was more than merely a rest time. This three day period is a recurring topic in scripture. When Ezra was getting ready to leave Babylon he gathered his people to the Ahava river, and there they abode in tents three days. (See notes on Ezra 8.) And now, once again, we see the same three day period in Nehemiah.

Our Lord said, reminding his hearers of Jonah the prophet, "As Jonah was three days and three nights in the whale's belly, so shall the Son of Man be three days and three nights in the heart of the earth." (Matt.12:40) This explains the meaning of the three day period. It brings us to the cross where Jesus bled and died. Our tendency is to think of the cross only in terms of sin; but we need to think of it also in terms of self. That Christ died for our sins is gloriously true, but He also died for us. And we need to learn that since conversion God has viewed us as having died in the death of Christ, and as having been raised again in the resurrection of Christ, so that we might walk with Him in newness of life.

Learning what that means in practical experience takes a lot of breaking and humbling. But until we learn the meaning of these things, we are as those who merely beat the air. Each of us must have our three days, so that we might be able to say with Paul, "Not I, but Christ."

"It is no longer I that liveth
It is Christ that liveth in me."

Nehemiah's secret exercise. (v. 12 - 16)

Nehemiah tells us how he went out to survey the city and to see for himself the work that needed to be done. He went out by the gate of the valley, and then on to the gate of the fountain. After that he went up by the brook, and there he viewed the wall, before returning by the valley gate. The scene that met his gaze must have been extremely depressing. In some places so much rubble had accumulated he found it quite impossible to pass.

But Nehemiah kept all this exercise to himself. "Neither told I any man what my God had put in my heart to do at Jerusalem." (v.12) "The rulers knew not where I went or what I did; neither had I as yet told it to the Jews, nor to the priests, nor to the nobles, nor to the rulers, nor to the rest who did the work." (v.16) We may therefore call the exercise of that night, 'Nehemiah's secret exercise'.

That this all happened in one night should not be overlooked. And what a momenteous night it was! It must have been, for Nehemiah, a sleepless night. He had encompassed the city, he had seen for himself the waste, he had been appalled at the debris. It was all just one sad story of reproach; the city where the Lord had chosen to put His name now lay in ruins. All who seek to be faithful in the service of God will know what it is to spend sleepless nights weeping over the state of the Lord's testimony in their midst. That they keep such exercises to themselves is understandable since there are so few who seem to care. But such exercises are inevitable where there are people of the calibre of Nehemiah.

Nehemiah reveals his plans (v. 17 - 20)

When the right time came Nehemiah evidently called all the people together. He wished to share with them his experience of the good hand of God upon him, how God had answered prayer and how He had wrought in the heart of the great king. And then, unburdening himself, he came immediately to the point, saying, "Let us build up the wall of Jerusalem." (v17)

It is very beautiful to note how the Lord seems to have been at work in the hearts of the people as well, for they immediately responded, and said "Let us arise and build" (v18). So they strengthened their hands for this good work. The implication of this statement seems to be that they strengthened each other's hands. The people encouraged one another and strengthened themselves and Nehemiah also felt strengthened. The scene described in these verses might remind us of the day of Pentecost when the believers "were all with one accord in one place." (Acts 2:1)

But the enemy was not far away. "When Sanballat and Tobiah heard, they laughed us to scorn and despised us." (v.19) Earlier we learned how their enemies were grieved when Nehemiah arrived in Jerusalem, but now we learn how they changed their approach and adopted the subtle tactic of ridicule. This is always a very difficult thing to handle and it often proves particularly effective when it is used against those who are young in the faith.

But Nehemiah teaches us how to handle it. He drew a sharp distinction between those who are on the Lord's side and those who are not. "The God of heaven will prosper us; therefore we will arise and build; but you have no portion, nor right, nor memorial in Jerusalem." (v.20) There are times when we must draw very firm lines. The best security for a believer, when he is faced with ridicule, is to interpose the Lord between himself and the foe, and to identify himself as clearly as he can on the Lord's side.

Faith enabled Nehemiah to do this. He was strong in faith and his faith was marked by intelligence, courage and wisdom. His recognition that a new day had dawned and that political power in the earth had passed into Gentile hands showed his intelligence. His robust attitude to Sanballet and Tobiah displayed his courage. And his wisdom was seen in the skilful way he devoted himself to the task of rebuilding the city walls of Zion.

LeT Us ArisE AnD BuilD

It is always a great temptation, when we come to a chapter, such as the one now before us, to leave it and go on to the next. To do so will invariably mean loss, because all scripture is given by inspiration of God, and is profitable. We should look upon this and similar chapters as sample pages from the book of life. (See also Ezra 2.) Such chapters show us the sorts of persons and the types of things, of which the Lord takes account. In these chapters we are permitted to glance over the shoulder of the recording angel and to learn the sobering truth that God's thoughts are not necessarily identical with our own.

We concluded our last chapter by noting the unity among the people of Jerusalem, now we are to see those same people acting as one in the building of the wall. Each group of workers was united in itself and all the groups were united to each other in the great task that lay before them. "Next unto him" and "next unto them" are recurring expressions in the first part of the chapter. While "after him" and "after them" are recurring expressions in the second part. The unifying factor was the wall and the singleminded desire of the people to see it rebuilt. Thus there was a remarkable solidarity of the workers with the work.

Going around the city

The chapter takes us on a complete and orderly circuit of the city, beginning with the Sheep gate and ending with the gate Miphkad, which was the last of the gates before we come back again to the Sheep gate. The Sheep gate was so called because through that gate the sheep were brought on their way to the temple and to the place of sacrifice. The name of the final gate was Miphkad. The word has, at its root, the idea of an assignment for which, eventually, an account must be given. The entire project was therefore bounded by these two gates.

We shall begin at the Sheep gate, and here it might be helpful for us to consider ourselves at the cross. And then we shall go right round the perimeter of the city until we come to the gate Miphkad. And at this final gate let us think of ourselves in the light of the coming again of our Lord Jesus Christ, since that is when we must all give account. For at His coming we must all appear before the judgement seat. The present age lies between these two great markers and the brief period of our pilgrimage through this world represents our season of responsibility and of service for the Master.

On one occasion our Lord likened Himself to a nobleman going into a far country, to obtain for himself a kingdom and to return. During his absence his goods were entrusted to his servants, with this charge, "Occupy till I come." Upon his return, he called those servants to see what each had gained by trading. Now our present position is akin to that of those servants during the time of their master's absence. It is therefore our urgent duty to attend to the Lord's interests, and to serve Him with all our hearts, so that when He comes we shall not be ashamed.

Former foes unite

It must be significant that the High Priest and his brethren took the lead in rebuilding the walls of the city. And it must be equally significant that the men of Jericho laboured next to them. Jericho was first brought before us as the people of Israel were beginning their conquest of the promised land. It was a heavily fortified city whose walls seemed to reach up to heaven. At that time the men of Jericho stood defiantly against Joshua and against the God of Israel. (See Joshua 6.) But now, we find them working in happy fellowship with the High Priest of their day.

This might carry us back in thought to our unconverted days when we too walked the road of life, in self-will and in disobedience, until God met us in saving grace. At that point and by the convicting work of the Holy Spirit and the miracle of regeneration we were brought into a wholly new relationship with Him and to-day we are the servants of the living and true God. This is our happy privilege; to serve a risen Saviour and to fill our hands with such service as is according to the will of God for us.

The entire chapter may be conveniently studied under two somewhat indivisible headings, the work and the workers. There was, as already noted, a great degree of unity in the work, but there was also a remarkable diversity, and the same was true of the workers. They stood together, shoulder to shoulder, and laboured as one man in the work, and that in spite of a wide diversity among them.

And herein lies an important principle. Diversity can work in unity, and unity can work in diversity. Our God is a God of variety: He is also a God of order. In the physical body there is great diversity among the members, and yet it is only as those diverse members work in harmony with one another, that the body can function as it was created to do.

The Work

The diversity in the work is immediately apparent, for we read that some built (v.1-3) while others repaired. (v.4-6) Sometimes in the work of God the only thing to do is to clear the decks and make a fresh start. We must begin from scratch. But at other times what is required is repair work. Indeed, the latter idea is more prominent than the former in the chapter before us. And this is what we would expect in that particular undertaking.

Our hearts are often heavy when we survey the Christian testimony, and especially the evangelical branch of it, and see it littered with casualties. There are so many who once made profession of Christ, and for a time ran well, who are now, in spiritual terms, like Jerusalem with its broken wall and its burned gates. There is a massive repair job waiting to be done. Where are the repairers who will search out and seek to recover the many over whom Satan has gained an undoubted advantage?

"Brethren, if a man (any man) be overtaken in some fault (any fault), you who are spiritual restore such a one in a spirit of meekness, considering yourself, lest you also be tempted." (See Gal.6:1.) Herein lies a test of our professed spirituality. In such an eventuality any who claim to be spiritual cannot be complacent or uncaring. Surely we need to recapture the spirit of Barnabas who sought out Saul of Tarsus, and led him from obscurity to become the foremost of all the Christian missionaries, and the role model for the church of God right down to our own day. (Acts 12:25)

Diversity of operations

Manifestly, the work was one, and yet it was also diverse in this sense, not everybody was assigned the same task. Some worked on the gates and some on the walls. Still others concentrated on the corners. Each task called for its own degree of skill. Those who could work on a straight part of the wall might not be suitable for turning a corner. And those who could do that, might have been found wanting if the task in hand was building one of the gates.

There is corresponding diversity among the gifts given by the Holy Spirit to believers. To some have been given several gifts, and to others only one. But no believer has been left without some ability to serve the Lord. Our duty is to stir up the gift that is in us and to exercise it, as God gives us opportunity. Someone, especially someone just setting out in the pathway of faith, might ask, how can I know my particular gift? The answer is quite simple. If we take the opportunities that come our way, and fill our hands with service for the Lord, it will soon emerge what it is that God has gifted us to do.

The Workers

Those in positions of trust and leadership should always be examples to others. And it was certainly praiseworthy that the priests led the way in building of the wall. (v.1) This was only as it should have been. It is no light thing to take a position of privilege among the Lord's people. Privilege always carries responsibility, and since no man lives to himself and no man dies to himself, we must ever be mindful of the influence our actions, or the lack of them, may have upon others.

After the priests, came the rulers (v.9,15) and then, after them, the Levites. (v.17) The goldsmiths and the perfumers are also mentioned. (v.8) Their regular work was of a fine and delicate nature, but even they put their hands to the task of building the wall. And besides the men, the women also found that there was work for them to do. The daughters of Shallum, the ruler of the half of Jerusalem, involved themselves in the work. (v.12)

And yet in the presence of such diversity, what marvellous unity prevailed at Jerusalem. We have already noted the repetition of expressions such as 'next to him' and 'next to them.' These and other similar expressions occur several times. Such expressions tell their own story. There was that independence which individual responsibility called forth, and yet at the same time there was that interdependence which was so necessary to the task. Anything else would have been quite inconsistent with their understanding of the will of the Lord.

Like the disciples on the day of Pentecost, the builders of Jerusalem's wall were all with one accord in one place. (Acts 2:1) And the effect was immediate. The gaps began to close and the breaches began to be made up until, eventually, the entire enterprise was carried to a successful and happy conclusion. The effort itself was a corporate one and by standing together the people shared in the blessing of God upon their labours.

The Nobles were Lukewarm

Some did their work with great thoroughness. Those who built or repaired the gates did not stop until beams and doors and locks and bars were all in place. (v.3,6) But others were somewhat lax. "Their nobles put not their necks to the work of their Lord." (v.5) The nobles feature often in this book, but seldom with credit. There is nothing like the power of a good example and the nobles were ideally placed to rouse and enthuse the rank and file of the people, but alas, they simply refused to be inconvenienced. The apostle James warns us of the danger of placing too much emphasis upon the nobles, that is, upon those who might come with their gold rings into the assembly of God's people.

It is a very modest observation, but one that we do well to underline, that some actually found their sphere of service just opposite to where they lived. "Jedaiah repaired, opposite his house." (v.10) And Benjamin and Hashub did the same. (See v.23.) In gospel work, the many are not called to 'climb the steeps and cross the waves,' their duty lies simply in climbing the steps across the street. And in any case, until we have proved ourselves in the Lord's service at home, it is unlikely that we shall be of much use for God on foreign soil. The first Christians were to begin their witness at Jerusalem, their home town. And the word to us all is, 'go home to your friends and tell them.'

Many more precious gems must be there to be gathered among the details recorded in this chapter. What a pity it would be to pass lightly over such a chapter and, as already alluded to, what loss to our souls. How we need eyes anointed by the Spirit of God that we might be enabled to see these precious things, hidden from the wise and prudent yet revealed unto babes.

And so the great enterprise was carried forward to the glory of God's name. And before long even their enemies had to acknowledge, "that the walls of Jerusalem were being made up, and that the breaches thereof were beginning to be closed." (Neh.4:7) And so, in the end, the wrath of men was made to praise the Lord.

TROUBLSOME TIMES

The next three chapters tell of the perils that beset Nehemiah in the great work to which he had put his hand. The chapter before us shows how he encountered both danger from without and discouragement from within. The Bible is a truly amazing book for its sacred histories are pertinent and relevant to us even in what we like to consider our sophisticated age. All who have ever borne any responsibility for the integrity of the Lord's testimony can easily identify with Nehemiah and the great issues with which he had to grapple.

Dangers from without

Even before the tremendous work of the previous chapter had been finished, the enemy was again on the scene. This is now the third time we have come across Sanballet and it is by no means the last. In these chapters the opposition Nehemiah faced came in at least seven different forms. The building of any other wall would have passed unnoticed but this was the city of God, and where God's interests are involved, there the enemy will always be found, active and perverse.

"It came to pass, when Sanballat heard that we were building the wall, he was angry, and felt great indignation, and mocked the Jews." (v.1) At the beginning, we saw how the enemy was grieved that there had come a man to seek the welfare of the people of God at Jerusalem. But now, having received the news of the rebuilding of the wall, he became angry and, a little later, when told how successful the builders had been, he became very angry. This intense and increasing anger was also mingled with contempt. And in all this Sanballat had the unswerving support of his faithful lieutenant, Tobiah the Ammonite.

On that previous occasion when Nehemiah encountered Sanballat, the latter had laughed him to scorn and despised the remnant of his people. 'Despised' simply means that he could not find a good word to say about Nehemiah and his people. But if his earlier target had been the workers it was now the work itself. "Even that which they build, if a fox go up, he shall break down their stone wall." (v.3)

Ridicule and mockery have always been subtle and devastating weapons in the arsenal of our great foe. Sarcasm and scorn, are perhaps, the most frequently used arrows in his quiver. He has used them again and again to great effect. Many have succumbed to them, and young believers have proved especially vulnerable to them. It is not easy for a new Christian to withstand the ribaldry of those who were once his friends. To be the butt of cruel jokes for the sake of Christ can be extremely trying. It must be significant that the scriptures expressly warn us that in the last days there will come scoffers. (2Peter 3:3)

Besides all this, Sanballat and Tobiah entered into a conspiracy with the Arabians, and the Ammonites, and the Ashdodites. These people formed part of the army of Samaria which was encamped nearby. The plan was that they would come against Jerusalem to hinder the work. The word 'hinder' is interesting, it means to cause a miscarriage. Their intention was to intervene in such a way that the entire project would be aborted.

All of these groups were at odds among themselves, yet they were united in a common opposition to Nehemiah and his builders. Some five hundred years later a similar coalition of darkness was brought together. The Pharisees and the Herodians, themselves bitter enemies, became uncommonly united in their hatred of God's Son. They conspired together and sought to undermine Him and, eventually, to destroy Him. (See Mark 3:6.)

Nehemiah Stands His Ground

The firm resolution displayed by Nehemiah in chapter two was now called forth once again. He said, "We made our prayer unto our God, and set a watch against them day and night." (v.9) Watch and pray were the watchwords given by the Lord to His disciples when He found them asleep in the garden of Gethsemane. (Mark 14:38) Setting a watch was important. God had put the builders in a position of responsibility and they recognised their duty by setting a watch. Failure to have done so would have been foolhardy and presumptuous. But having done so, they were now able to discharge their tasks in complete dependence upon their God. That is what prayer meant for them in that somewhat unique situation.

It is an interesting detail that Nehemiah placed a watch in two locations. First in the hollows, the lower places behind the wall, and then, secondly, in the higher places.(v.13) For our part, we should remember that life itself is cast between these two extreme positions. We are forever vulnerable when on our high places. "Let him who thinks he stands, take heed lest he fall." (1Cor.10:12) At the same time, we must not be careless about the dangers inherent in our valley experiences.

Scripture records for us a fascinating account of the two Syrian campaigns fought by Ahab, who was king in Samaria some years before. The account serves to illustrate the meaning of the watch set by Nehemiah. After Ahab had gained his first victory, we are told that there came a man of God with this message for the king, "Because the Syrians have said, The Lord is God of the hills, but He is not God of the valleys, therefore will I deliver all this great multitude into your hand, and you shall know that I am the Lord." (1 Ki.20:28)

Both in valley situations and on our high places we should never forget that our God rules over all. He is God of the valleys as well as of the hills. The sacred history lists many who in the presence of danger found their refuge in the Lord and in the place of prayer. Jehosaphat and Hezekiah were examples of this before the captivity and now we have Nehemiah after it. The danger may at times be more or less, but the believer's strong tower is always the same.

In seasons of testing, the godly also have an inclination to turn to the book of Psalms to find solace and strength. Nehemiah's prayer might suggest, that at this time he was dwelling a good deal in those Psalms known as the songs of degrees, the first of which is the 120th. Danger and deliverance are the two themes of those Psalms. Facing danger in an immediate and extreme form Nehemiah made his prayer unto God. His prayer was wonderfully answered and he was marvellously delivered.

At that time the Lord strengthened his hands, and the hands of his people in an extraordinary way. We read that "the people had a mind to work" and "so we built the wall, and all the wall was joined together to half of its height." (v.6) This remarkable result was yet another example of the preserving and overruling hand of God, upon a work that was according to His will and for His glory. And it demonstrated to the remnant how God can make the wrath of man to praise Him.

Discouragements from within

Difficulties from without we can and do expect, but when they come from within the fellowship of the church they are always of a wholly different order. And yet, what Nehemiah now experienced has been the lot of God's servants throughout the ages. Paul, the apostle, summed up the vexations that we so often experience when he wrote, "without were fightings and within were fears." (2Cor.7:5)

There was a great deal of rubbish, and this made construction work much more difficult. The stones would first need to be dug out of the rubbish and then the rubbish itself cleared away. This was tedious and time consuming and it became a cause of frustration and of discouragement to the builders.

Rubbish of one kind or another has a tendency to accumulate in church life and in the hearts of church members. Invariably it gives rise to dissension which in turn brings discouragement to godly souls. In this matter we need to judge ourselves. We must first sanctify Christ as Lord and then endeavour to bring everything into captivity to the mind of Christ.

In addition, there were those Jews whose lot was to live among the adversaries. They had their ear to the ground, and to their great consternation they learned of a conspiracy against Jerusalem. The enemy would assemble his combined force and come and destroy the good work that had been so painstakingly done. The attack, when it came, could be from any quarter and it would have the element of suprise. Not once or twice, but ten times this intelligence was brought to Nehemiah. What credence should he attach to it. Was it simply hearsay?

Remember the Lord

Nehemiah's reaction was quite superb. It was a considered and calm demonstration of a living faith in the living God. Besides setting a watch he gave the people a battle cry, "Remember the Lord." (v.14) He interposed the Lord between himself and the foe. In the end, this is the one thing needful. Leave the Lord out and defeat is certain, but bring the Lord into the situation and victory is secure. This is what Moses meant when he charged Israel saying, "Beware, that thou forget the Lord." (Deut.8:11)

Historically, there were many times when Israel did just that, they forgot the Lord. Take, as an example, the memorable valley of Elah when Goliath of Gath defied the living God, and Saul and his armies were powerless to do anything about it. The reason for their weakness was their failure to bring the Lord into the equation. In the record, the Lord is not even mentioned until late in the day when David arrived on the scene. But David immediately brought the Lord in. He said, "The Lord who delivered me out of the paw of the lion, and out of the paw of the bear, He will deliver me out of the hand of this Philistine." (See 1Sam.17:37.) The history tells of a notable victory won that day.

At this point Nehemiah and his people were, in a sense, right back at Kadesh Barnea (Numbers 13) The men of Judah who lived among the adversaries, were as the ten spies who brought back an evil report of the land. Those spies had completely lost sight of the Lord. Their preoccupation had been with the inhabitants of the land, who seemed like gaints, and also with their own feebleness for they said, we were like grasshoppers in their sight. The effect of their report had been to discourage the people, and the net result was that thirty eight years of wandering in the wilderness followed until all that generation apart from Caleb and Joshua had died. Happily, Nehemiah kept his eye on God and a situation with much potential for disaster was redeemed.

Nehemiah proved that "God is the rewarder of them that diligently seek Him." (Hebs.11:6) He saw his enemies thwarted. They too had heard a report for it was reported to them that their plans were known in Jerusalem and that God had brought their counsel to nothing. (v.15) And then, in addition, the crisis yielded fruit that fell to Nehemiah's advantage.

The Fruits of Righteousness

An extreme situation called for extreme measures, and the returned exiles were not found wanting. They redoubled their efforts. Apart from washing, they did not put off their clothes. Half of the people worked while the other half watched, and special arrangements were made to cover the hours of darkness. The people laboured together, with a weapon in one hand and a tool in the other, and so the work went forward and prospered.

Special mention is made of the Trumpeter who stood by Nehemiah at that time. All the people were exhorted to keep their ears tuned to the sound of the trumpet. "The work is great and large, and we are separated upon the wall, one far from another. In what place therefore you hear the sound of the trumpet, resort thither unto us, our God shall fight for us." (v.19,20)

This trumpet, like the silver trumpets in the wilderness, (see Numbers 10) seems to suggest the corporate subjection of the people to the word of God. Salvation is always an individual matter; "if any man enter in he shall be saved." But Christianity is essentially a corporate matter. The people of God are one. And the ultimate test of our profession and of our love for Christ is our attitude to His word. "If you love me, keep my commandments." (John 14:15)

When God calls His people to endure buffetings we can be sure that He has spiritual blessing in store for them. It may be, the people of Jerusalem were becoming complacent and, consequently, the work may have been suffering. But now, the wrath of man was made to praise the Lord, and whatever the internal difficulties, they were overcome.

The result was that a new sense of unity and of urgency seized the people and with it a mind to work so that the purpose of God might be realised. Nehemiah and his people went on and pressed forward in their great task. Together they present a beautiful illustration of what should be the normal state of the church, "Always abounding in the work of the Lord." (1Cor.15:58)

STRIFE WITHIN THE GATES

Two rather special things need to be said about the chapter that now lies before us. The first is that in its beginning it records the first real trouble to arise from within the Jerusalem congregation of that time. In the previous chapter the people had known discouragement, and they had successfully overcome it. But here Nehemiah finds himself on the offensive against the rulers and nobles of his own people. The second thing is that at its close this chapter expresses the potential for good that one man may have whose life is truly governed by the fear of God.

Three companies need to be distinguished in these verses. First, there was the multitude of the people, secondly, the rulers and nobles and, finally, Nehemiah himself and his closest associates. Each group has its own very important message for us.

The great work of building the wall was charged upon all the people. And to their lasting credit it has to be said, that they gave themselves to the task without reserve. And so the work went on and prospered, for we are told that the people had a mind to work. In fact, the point is reached in this chapter where the wall was actually joined together even to half its height.

In this age, our project is not the city walls of Zion, but the church of the living God. Jesus said, "I will build my church, and the gates of hell shall not prevail against it." (Matt.16:18) Responsibility for this great undertaking is enjoined upon all who are truly the Lord's. And, of course, there is a work for each of us to do in the furtherance of that purpose. Failure at this point will surely earn the Lord's censure at the time of His coming again. While faithfulness will be rewarded with His "well done good and faithful servant."

But such devoted service is costly, just as it was in Nehemiah's day. Those were difficult times in Jerusalem. Not only did grievous famine conditions exist but the people had been forced to neglect their normal occupations because of the urgency of the wall. Moreover, in order to feed their families, some even had to mortgage their houses and lands, while others were forced to borrow what money they could, using what possessions they had as security.

Many to-day are ready to serve, provided they do not have a price to pay, but true service is always costly. Many years ago, when he was preparing the materials for the building of the first temple, David was moved to ask, "Shall I render unto the Lord that which cost me nothing?" The ancient ceremonial law insisted that the offerings had to be without blemish. We fear that many are like those referred to by the prophet Malachi, who are content to offer unto the Lord the modern equivalent of the lame and the sick. (See Mal.1:8.)

We need to recover an understanding of this, that only our very best is suitable to be offered to the Lord. That is the reason why service for God can be such a costly matter. And those seeking to engage in any form of full time Christian service, either at home or abroad, should be ready for sacrifice. The people of Jerusalem had come all the way from Babylon to perform a very special task and they did not shrink from the sacrifice that task involved.

The Nobles and the Rulers

But now an almost unbelievable scenario is brought to light. "There was a great cry of the people and of their wives against their brethren, the Jews." (v.1) When he came to Jerusalem at the beginning Nehemiah had released many of the people from certain forms of bondage that had been incurred because of some debt. (v.8) But now, to his very great displeasure, he found the nobles and rulers of the people exploiting, for their own ends, the plight of the builders. They were actually bringing their brethren again into bondage

The nobles were enriching themselves by exacting an exorbitant interest from the people. Such activity was not only contrary to the spirit of the occasion it was also a clear breach of the letter of the law. (See Lev.25:35-39.) The exploitation of the poor is a practice overtly common in many lands to-day and covertly in others. Besides being roundly condemned in scripture it will come under the sure judgement of God. (See Jas.5:1-6.) But when such a malignancy is found among those who themselves claim to be numbered among the redeemed of the Lord it raises very serious and fundamental questions.

In the actual building of the wall these same nobles had already shown themselves more than a little work shy. (See ch.3:5.) Before long we shall see them again, this time in league with the enemy. (See ch.6:17.) But here we learn that they were possessed of a spirit of crass materialism. What did it matter if their brethren were impoverished so long as they could be enriched? The love of money, when it takes possession of a man, tends to make him callous and uncaring. The example before us of the pernicious effect of the materialistic spirit should be carefully pondered by us all.

Nehemiah tells us that he was very angry when he heard the cry of the people. He says, "I consulted with myself, and I rebuked the nobles, and the rulers." (v.7) How long he spent consulting with himself we are not told, but we can be quite sure that, as on so many other occasions, he again made his prayer to God. He did not react in the heat of the moment, nor did he speak unadvisedly. But satisfied of his own rectitude he knew he was in a strong position to deal with the offenders, even though they were the nobles and the rulers of the people.

In all this we should learn an important lesson from this man of God. Before we judge others, if we took a little time to judge ourselves, many a situation would turn out differently. Nehemiah knew exactly what he must do and he had the courage to do it. He called a great assembly and laid charges against the wrongdoers. He brought home to them the grievous evil of which they were guilty. And he pressed the charges home until arrows of conviction pierced the hard hearts of these men.

God graciously granted repentance on the part of the nobles. For in the presence of the priests, who acted as witnesses, they covenanted to make restitution and to restore the situation as far as they could. Taking a leaf from Ezekiel's book, Nehemiah then gave them an enacted parable. He shook out his lap, and said, "So God shake out every man from his house, and from his labour, that performs not this promise, even thus be he shaken out, and emptied." (v.13) A resounding 'Amen' by the congregation put a seal upon the whole affair.

The Materialistic Spirit

What the real character of the closing days of this present age will be is a much debated topic. One thing seems clear. The Laodicean issue will be the burning issue of the end of the age. "Rich, and increased with goods, and in need of nothing..." (Rev.3:17) Materialism will be, and indeed already is, the great issue of the last days of this present church age. It may very well be that our obsession with the question of ecumenism has allowed the enemy to outsmart us. For it is materialism and not ecumenism that is having such a debilitating effect upon today's testimony.

The first real trouble in Israel, after Joshua led the people over Jordan, had materialism at its heart. Achan saw, and coveted, and took, the wedge of gold and the goodly Babylonian garment. (See Josh. ch.7.) And again, at the very beginning of the Christian church the first intervention of God in judgement was occasioned by this same spirit of materialism. Ananias and Saphira conspired together to keep back part of the price and thus they lied to the Holy Ghost.

And here in the chapter before us we learn that the love of money lay behind the first contentious issue to raise its head among the people of God at Jerusalem. Money itself is neither godly or ungodly, it is neutral, but the love of money is the root of all evil. And that this is a great evil to-day is most manifest. Its pernicious operation in the lives of church members is resulting in great weakness in the work and witness of the church itself.

Nehemiah and those close to him

The closing section of the chapter introduces us to a happier scene. Nehemiah personally, and those near to him are found in marked and dignified contrast to the nobles and rulers of Jerusalem. Nehemiah is constrained to give a brief, interim report of his stewardship as Governor of the city. And it is a good report. The most salient thing in it is the way Nehemiah saw his own role. He saw himself as one who had come to Jerusalem not to be ministered unto, but to minister. His concern, therefore, was expressed in terms of giving rather than of getting.

We cannot but be impressed by the emphasis on the negatives in the closing verses of this chapter. "I and my brethren have not eaten the bread of the Governor." Former Governors did...but so did not I." "Neither bought we any land" etc. (See vv.14-18.) This reminds us of our Lord's teaching on self-denial. He said, "If any man will come after me, let him deny himself, and take up his cross daily, and follow me." (Luke 9:23)

Splendid Example of Self-Denial

Here is a principle found throughout scripture. Anything that may be accounted of value in the spiritual realm usually involves a denial of self in one form or another. Moses refused to be called the son of Pharaoh's daughter. Paul counted the things that were gain, to be but loss. And our Lord humbled Himself, and made Himself of no reputation. It might be safely said that if what we are doing for the Lord does not involve some element of self sacrifice it is doubtful if it is worth doing at all.

Nehemiah, for his part, did not take up his option to cream off 'the food of the people,' that is, the levy that was due to him as Governor. His predecessors had done nothing wrong in appropriating to themselves what was their due, but Nehemiah did not do so. (v.14,15) Nor did he allow any otherwise lawful pursuit, like speculating in land deals, to divert him from the great task of building the wall. Moreover, it would seem that those who were close to him, and who shared his confidence, were of the same mind as Nehemiah himself in these things. (v.16)

And yet his hospitality was lavish. Besides the many guests from the surrounding territories who daily shared his table, he entertained one hundred and fifty of his own people on a daily basis, dining them at his own table. This required enormous provision, yet he maintained the integrity of his resolve, not to burden the people, even though he might have done so as of right. (v.18) Unlike the nobles and the rulers, with whom he contended, he would not have the people to feel oppressed by any action he might take. Nehemiah proved God in marvelleous ways and showed to his people, and to us, the great truth that our God can supply all our need.

The final verse is a prayer and a consolation. "Think upon me, my God, for good, according to all that I have done for this people." (v.19) Nehemiah did not seek the approbation of men but the well done of God. If the people had failed to appreciate or even to acknowledge what he had done for them, he was comforted by the knowledge that all was manifest in the sight of Him with whom we all have to do.

THE TESTING
OF NEHEMIAH

We must not miss the significance of what is brought before us at this point. Following the reference to Nehemiah's personal integrity at the end of the last chapter, we are now once again, and quite predictably, confronted by the enemy. We say quite predictably for this has been the pattern in every age. Think of how it was in our Lord's time. Immediately after His baptism when the Father had borne audible witness to Him saying, "This is my beloved Son in whom I am well pleased" (Matt.3:17) Jesus was led out into the wilderness where He was tempted of the Devil.

The same scenario can be seen in the book of Job. God said, "Have you considered my servant Job, that there is none like him in all the earth." (Job1:8) Then there followed the mysterious testing of Job. Mysterious, both to Job himself and to all who were around him. Among the many things the story of Job teaches us, one thing stands out clearly; the adversary may be very powerful, he is not all-powerful, for God put a hedge around Job and Satan could only touch him as God allowed. But the principle seen in both Jesus and Job holds to this present time and we too find that times of blessing are often followed by times of testing.

The Wiles of the Devil

The enemy was first brought before us in chapter two. There he made just a single assault against the returned exiles and their great enterprise. In chapter four his activity was stepped up for he made two attacks. But in this chapter he asserts himself several times. This chapter, therefore, marks a very great intensification of enemy activity. Moreover, the enemy's attention is here directed towards Nehemiah personally, whereas earlier he simply opposed the work or at most the corporate leadership. But, at this point, Nehemiah is compelled to contend directly with the enemy in no fewer than six separate instances.

In addition, a very significant milestone is reached in this chapter for here we are told that the wall was finished in the twenty and fifth day of the month Elul, in fifty two days. (v.15) Some have argued that such an immense task could not have been completed in this time frame. But two factors must to be taken into account. First, the vast number of workers, their zeal for the work and also their skills. And second, the fact that the materials were already to hand, the stones simply had to be raised from the rubble which lay around the circumference of the city.

The completion of the wall in this record time means that the events recorded in this chapter must have taken place during the last days of the building. The very timing of this latest opposition, therefore, combined with its increasing intensity serves to emphasise lessons of deep importance to us. How often believers are warned in scripture of the hostile nature of the last days. "In the last days perilous times shall come." (2Tim.3:1) There would appear to be commanding evidence on every hand that the last days of the present age are already upon us.

While the several events of this chapter undoubtedly have many pertinent lessons to teach, we can discern that behind the activities detailed for us there were three really significant issues that forced themselves upon Nehemiah. The first was compromise, the second slander and the third presumption.

Compromise

Having tried frivolity and then the threat of force the enemy now resorted to an offer of friendship. Sanballat sent a message inviting Nehemiah to meet him in one of the villages in the plain of Ono. (v.2) But Nehemiah had no difficulty in recognising this proffered friendship to be feigned for the enmity behind it was only thinly veiled. Wisdom dictated that Nehemiah should be both cautious and suspicious, he said, "They thought to do me mischief." Many believe their purpose was to kidnap and imprison Nehemiah and perhaps even to kill.

The reply he sent back was superb. "I am doing a great work, so that I cannot come down. Why should the work cease, while I leave it, and come down to you?" (v.3) Two things stand out. First, there is the emphasis upon the work. This was God's work and anything that might hinder or impair the work of God must be avoided. The enemy has targeted the work of God in our day as well and is, as we have noted, engaged in an unrelenting struggle to frustrate it.

And then, besides the practical difficulty pleaded by Nehemiah, which was quite genuine, there was also a spiritual and moral dimension to his reply. There was the need for Nehemiah to come down if he would accede to Sanballat's invitation. Nehemiah occupied the high ground, but now he was being invited to come down to the same level as his opponents. In the eyes of many this would have suggested a compromise with the enemy and a lowering of standards.

If that was so, it was not new, for such a suggestion has always been a common tactic of the evil one. Where will God's standards be maintained if not in the church? And yet, is it not just there that a most serious erosion of the divine patterns is in evidence. It is all too common for those who would faithfully maintain divine order in the house of God, to find themselves ridiculed and set at naught, with a consequent temptation to lower sound biblical standards. All such have a great deal to encourage them in Nehemiah.

Let us be clear about this, God has His standards, they are revealed in His word, and it is our absolute duty to uphold them even in the presence of an adversary who will not give up easily. Four times the subtle invitation was sent to Nehemiah. Each time he answered them after the same manner. "I cannot come down." It is the only way! We must be strong in the Lord and then when the enemy has done all he can against us, we shall stand fast in the Lord and in the power of His might.

Slander

But where one tactic fails the enemy has another. Following the failure of a suggested compromise, Nehemiah soon became the object of slander. How relevant the scriptures are to every generation. Inuendo, hearsay and talebearing are common weapons in Satan's armoury. Like Zerubbabel, his illustrious predecessor, Nehemiah too, was to become the victim of an open letter.

Open letters in those days were a kind of calculated insult. They were not unlike political leaks by government departments today. Their poisonous effect was to sow reports of what was only an assumed evil. In this case they wrote, "It is reported among the nations, and Gashmu says it (Gashmu was apparently considered an authority in these matters), that you and the Jews think to rebel: for which cause you build the wall, that you may be their king" (v.6)

They considered that this was sufficient ground to force Nehemiah to come down. They said, "Come now therefore, and let us take counsel together." (v.7) But once again Nehemiah returned an uncompromising reply. He did not panic and he certainly did not parley, he simply said, "There are no such things done as you say, but you devise them out of your own heart." (v.8) Their words were evil imaginings, inventions of perverted minds, seeking to frustrate the work of God and to tarnish the good name of His honoured servant.

The Talebearer

Talebearing is a great evil. It is a subtle and malicious form of slander. Those who are guilty of it should know that the same sinister and shadowy enemy is working in them who also worked in Sanballat, Tobiah and Geshem. Alas, some who would be most scrupulous about their own image have sometimes been guilty of spreading unfounded and specious rumours about some servant of the Lord to the great detriment of the work of God. The evil of giving our lips to talebearing is equalled only by giving our ears to it. Let us beware!

The law stated, "You shall not go up and down as a talebearer among my people." (Lev.19:16) Later, Solomon declared "a talebearer reveals secrets, but a faithful spirit conceals the matter." And again, "The words of a talebearer are as wounds, they go down into the innermost parts." And yet again, "Where no wood is, the fire goes out: so where no talebearer is, the strife ceases." (See Prov.11:13, 18:8, 26:20.)

The tongue may be a little member but it is a world of iniquity. Like feathers driven by the wind, words spoken in malice cannot be recalled. It is impossible to calculate the harm that has been done, both to individual believers and to corporate companies of the saints, by slanderous reports put about by ill disposed persons.

In this context, we cannot emphasise too much the example that Nehemiah has left us. It was by prayer he met all the malice and spite that was levelled against him. "Now therefore, O God, strengthen my hands." (v.9) This was just one of a whole series of impulse prayers recorded in this book. Nehemiah was a man who enjoyed such intimacy with the Lord, he could turn and speak to the

Lord on the instant about whatever issue arose. He seems to have been a man, like Moses, to whom the Lord could speak face to face.

Surely here is a facility we would do well to cultivate, for the difficulties Nehemiah faced have their counterpart in every believer's experience. We can do no better, in the presence of some provocation, than to turn to the Lord and bring the issue to Him in prayer.

Presumption

The third attack of the enemy was even more subtle than the others. Nehemiah tells us how he came to the house of Shemaiah who said to him, "Let us meet together in the house of God, in the temple, and let us shut the doors, for they will come to slay you." (v.10) The notion behind this suggestion was that Nehemiah should make an improper use of the house of God. That he should actually use the temple of God to save his own skin.

Shemaiah is said to have been shut up which some take to mean that he was shut out from the temple because of some ceremonial uncleanness found in him. If this was so, then for Nehemiah to have gone to the temple in the company of Shemaiah, would have exposed him to a charge of breaking the very law he professed to maintain. For the law of Moses certainly did exclude people from the temple in specific circumstances of uncleanness. To have done what had been suggested would have been wrong in itself. To have done so in association with Shemaiah would only have compounded the wrong.

But again, Nehemiah's response was weighty. He said, "Should such a man as I flee...or go into the temple to save his life. I will not go in." When this is read alongside his responses to the earlier testings, it is not difficult to see in Nehemiah a Mr Greatheart. He stood for truth and for God and God honoured him for the stand he took. But he did not stand in any spirit of pretentious boasting. On the contrary, his attitude was always one of humble dependence upon his God. Once more in this chapter we hear him in prayer, with his heart lifted heavenward he prays, "My God, think thou upon Tobiah and Sanballat according to these their works." (v.14)

And so the wall was finished. (v.15) Although the people of the nations around Jerusalem were dismayed at the finish of the work, they had to admit that what had been done, and the very manner in which it was done, was wrought of God. Such was the testimony, however grudging, of the heathen world. How sad then that in the last three verses of the chapter, we read again of the nobles of the people, this time, acting as a kind of fifth column.

They were in league with the enemy, exchanging letters with Tobiah. When speaking to Nehemiah they always had a good word to say about Tobiah, but when speaking to Tobiah they never seemed to have anything good to say of Nehemiah. This treachery had its roots in the problem of mixed marriages. Tobiah was the son in law of Shechaniah and his son Johanan was married to the daughter of Meshullam. The matter is simply noted in this chapter but later we shall learn the action taken by Nehemiah to deal with it. (See Chapter 13.)

Be not unequally yoked together with unbelievers is the exhortation of Paul the apostle. The implications for a believer, of an unequal yoke especially in a marriage covenant, can be far reaching indeed. And when this practice becomes acceptable in any assembly of Christians it will not be long until important issues will be judged, not on the basis of the principles raised, but on the basis of the personalities involved.

ADMISSION TO ZION

This chapter records the final acts of Nehemiah before his temporary absence from Jerusalem. He did come back again some time later and put in order certain other things. (See Ch.13:6,7.) But for the present the wall had been built, the doors set up and the porters or gate keepers appointed. Very strict instructions were also given about who might, and who might not, enter the holy city. Great care was to be taken in this matter.

Responsibility for guarding the gates was committed to faithful men. Hanani was Nehemiah's brother. We heard from him at the beginning when he reported to Nehemiah the sad state of Jerusalem. (See Ch.1:1,2.) And now he is given a most solemn charge. Some see just one man in verse two, and take the name Hanani to be a shortened form of Hananiah. If this is so the verse would read, "I gave to my brother, Hanani, even Hananiah..." Assuming this to have been the case, it follows that the descriptive part of the verse is a description of Nehemiah's brother.

Evidently Hanani had already proved himself as the keeper of the adminstrative area, called the palace, which was to the north of the temple site. (v.2) Now he is given added responsibility by being put in charge of the entire city for the period of his brother's absence. He is described as a faithful man, and one who feared God more than many. He presents a telling illustration of the principle that God entrusts with greater honour those who have proved themselves faithful in that which is lesser. The fear of the Lord is the beginning of wisdom. And it was just there that Hanani began for he had a deep and becoming reverence for the God who had chosen Jerusalem as the place where He would put His name.

A Faithful Man

The appointment of Hanani also illustrates the instruction Paul gave to Timothy regarding the truth committed to him. "The things that you have heard from me among many witnesses, the same commit to faithful men, who shall be able to teach others also." (2Tim.2:2) There is a pressing need today for men of this calibre among God's people. Modern society glorifies success, how it may have been achieved seems secondary, but God's concern is still for faithfulness.

Ultimate and absolute faithfulness is seen only in God Himself. Faithfulness in God quite simply means that He is true to His word. Having given us His word God is not indifferent to that word. And so when we take our stand upon the promises of God we are standing on promises that can never fail, if it were otherwise God would cease to be God. Democratic votes may fairly reflect the opinions of men, but our final court of appeal must always be to the good word of God.

It follows that those who stand for God must aim, above all else, to have this character that they too are true to their word. Above all other men, a believer's word must be his bond. This must surely be the first expression of practical holiness. Nor should we think that faithfulness is either easily or cheaply come by. Faithfulness required

Abraham to lay his only son on the altar of sacrifice. It constrained
Esther to lay her very life on the line. It cost Stephen a martyr's
death while Peter had to pay the same price. And yet the call of God
to all His people remains, "Be thou faithful unto death, and I will
give thee a crown of life." (Rev.2:10)

Hanani was faithful and feared God more than others. When all
is said and done, faithfulness on our part can only be a relative matter,
and it is important that we recognise this to be the case. The
recognition of this relative principle will develop in us both a
becoming humility, and a ready grace to defer to another brother's
greater discernment. In this area none of us has already attained, but
we press towards the goal of an ever greater degree of faithfulness
to God and to His word.

Who can enter Zion

The burning issue in the chapter before us was admission to, or
exclusion from, the city of God. The porters or gate keepers are
addressed and instructed in their duty. The gates were not to be opened
before a certain hour and then they were to be closed again before
nightfall. And while this was being done guards were to be standing
by at strategic points. (v.3) The spiritual significance of all this must
have a great bearing upon the ordering of the affairs of every Christian
church.

The broad principle was simple enough. Those who came by day
could enter, those who came by night could not. (v.3) It is not
inconceivable that Paul may have had this very instruction in mind
when he drew such a sharp distinction between the children of the
day, who are believers, and the children of the night, who are
unbelievers.(See 1Thess.5:5.) In a day and at a time when the frontiers
of light and darkness are increasingly blurred, it is important to
remember that God still puts the same necessary distinction between
the church and the world.

The basic principle of receiving new people into any fellowship
of believers is also equally simple. "Receive one another, as Christ

also has received you to the glory of God." (Rom.15:7) There is always a tendency, especially on the part of legalistic brethren, to erect barriers to fellowship that are manifestly not of God. This has the effect of rending the body of Christ and of doing untold harm to sincere believers, many of whom may be young in the faith, and perhaps deeply impressionable.

In our zeal we might just forget that faithfulness to the Lord has its counterpart in faithfulness to His people. And where the former is found the latter will certainly not be wanting. We should always have in mind the words of our Saviour, "Inasmuch as you have done it unto one of the least of these my brethren, you have done it unto me." (Matt. 25:40) Those charged with this responsibility do well to be cautious as Nehemiah was cautious, and yet they must be extremely vigilant that they do not refuse those whom Christ has already received.

Proving ourselves

On the other hand, all who seek to identify themselves with any local fellowship should recognise that they have a duty to give creditable evidence that they are truly the Lord's. The apostle John wrote of some, "They went out from us, for they were not of us; for if they had been of us, they would no doubt have continued with us; but they went out, that they might be made manifest that they were not all of us." (1John 2:19)

Believers are in the world but they are not of it, and we must recognise the force of this. On the other hand, unbelievers are not of the church and when they find themselves in it, the consequences can be disastrous, not only for themselves but also for the prosperity of that particular church. The need for a careful watch is just as great today as it was at Jerusalem in Nehemiah's day. Otherwise the already long casualty lists, which are such a reproach upon the Christian community, will become even longer.

Nor are we left to our own personal preferences or prejudices in this important matter, for whatever other grounds there may be for the exercise of godly discipline in the church, the two grounds for exclusion from the fellowship are clearly identified in the New Testament. The first is doctrinal error. "If there come any unto you, and bring not this doctrine, receive him not into your house, neither bid him godspeed; for he who bids him godspeed is partaker of his evil deeds." (2John 10,11)

The other ground is moral evil. "But now I have written unto you not to keep company, if any man that is called a brother be a fornicator...put away from yourselves that wicked person." (1Cor.5:11-13) A hearty love of truth and a solid commitment to purity of life are the two great evidences, that will give credibility to the testimony of any who seek to join a given fellowship of God's people. These are the two immediate things that will commend us to the fellowship of others who love our Lord Jesus Christ in sincerity. The absence of one or other of these great evidences should give rise to godly exercise and very great caution.

The Register

The remainder of our chapter is taken up with the register of those who came up at the first, who came up with Zerrubbabel. The total number registered is as already found in Ezra 2 (see our comments on that chapter), but some of the names are different. Critics might point to this as a discrepancy, but there may be a very simple explanation. It was quite common in Bible times, as it is today, for a person to be known by more than one name. For instance, Peter, the apostle, had three names, he was also called Simon and Cephas.

Even where the figures differ, it might be that one list gives the number who enlisted to go, while the other the number who actually travelled. Moreover, the differences could even be viewed as an evidence of inspiration. Had some human mind been seeking to falsify the records, the obvious thing would have been to make the two lists look totally alike. Differences of this nature do not in the least cloud our view of the infallibility and integrity of the sacred scriptures.

Doubtful Persons

Attention is called, as in Ezra 2, to the fact that some presented themselves whose pedigree was open to dispute. "They could not show their father's houses, nor their seed, whether they were of Israel." (v.61) Great prudence was needed in handling such a situation. The way forward was clearly to give such people time to prove themselves, so that their title to be numbered with the others could be firmly established.

Some even claimed the right of priesthood who could not verify their claim without some degree of doubt. Nehemiah ruled that until a priest using the Urim and Thummim could pronounce a judgement, their claim too must be held in abeyance. The Urim and the Thummim, meaning light and perfection, were two stones which were contained in the breastplate of the high priest. They were used to discern the mind of the Lord in certain given situations. The purpose of the stones is now supplied by the scriptures, for the Lord guides His people today by His word.

But when it comes to the material offerings that were given by the people there is a marked difference between the record of this chapter and what we have in Ezra 2. And here again, the explanation may be simple. Both records tell us what some gave and Nehemiah records more of the some than Ezra. He even records what he himself gave in his capacity as the Tirshatha or Governor of the people. (vv. 68-73)

The last verse really begins the story of the next chapter. It is a simple statement of achievement, a record of what God had done in the midst of His people. In spite of all the opposition encountered over the twelve years covered by the book up to this point, "The priests, and the Levites, and the porters, and the singers, etc. dwelt in their cities; and when the seventh month came the children of Israel were in their cities." (v.73) God had been with them and had made their way prosperous. Nehemiah's mission was complete.

BrinG The BooK

A new section of the book begins with this chapter. The wall had been restored but that was largely a material and mundane exercise. The question that now arose concerned the moral and spiritual condition of the people. Every true revival involves, besides the restoration of things that may have broken down, a moral reformation among the people who are affected by it. We have considered the building up of Zion's wall, now we must think about the building up of Zion's people.

This, and the following chapter record three very notable gatherings of the people. First they assembled together for a reading of God's word. (8:1) Then they came together to observe the feast of Tabernacles. (8:13) And finally they met again for a day of humiliation and prayer. (9:1) They heard the word with the hearing of faith. Then they studied with great care the detail of that word and, finally, they brought themselves under its power and authority.

It is interesting that these meetings all occurred in the seventh month; that was the month God had ordained for the people to assemble at Jerusalem to keep the last three of the seven annual feasts. And it may be that parallels can be drawn between those three final feasts, Trumpets, Atonement and Tabernacles, (see Lev.23.) and the events before us in these chapters.

Meeting No 1

At the first meeting a wonderful sense of unity was again in evidence, "All the people gathered themselves together as one man." (v.1) In the record of that memorable assembly there are at least ten references to 'all the people'. This is more than could be said at the time of the building of the wall for then there were some who held back. That they should have come together in this way reminds us of the Psalmist's fine description of godly oneness, "Behold, how good and how pleasant it is for brethren to dwell together in unity! For there the Lord commanded the blessing, even life for evermore." (Psa.133:1,3)

Ezra now appears for the first time in this book. Some have inferred that he is not mentioned until this point because he was absent from Jerusalem during the period covered by the earlier chapters. But the silence may simply emphasise that Ezra and Nehemiah were quite different men, with different qualities and gifts.

Building the wall was quite clearly the forte of Nehemiah, but now the issue is the moral state of the people and Ezra's gifts in this area brings him to the fore. Nehemiah was a great leader and an able administrator, he was skilled in co-ordinating and carrying through any enterprise to which he put his hand. But Ezra was a ready scribe in the law of his God, and he was eminently fitted to bring God's word to bear upon heart and conscience, and this he did with compelling effect.

A Great Bible Reading

As one man, the people called upon Ezra to "bring the Book," the book of the law of Moses, which the Lord had commanded to Israel. (v.1) We take this to mean the Pentateuch, which the Jews call the Torah, the Law. Then with great solemnity he opened the book, (v.5) and then they read in the book, in the law of God. (v.8) It seems that this matter of Bible reading actually became a habit with the people. (See also Ch.8:18,9:3 & Ch.13:1.) Regrettably, the prevailing habit today seems to be the neglect of this basic and important exercise; the regular reading of God's word.

We have already stated that a good test of anything that passes for revival, or that claims in any sense to be revival, is to ask, "What place does it give to the word of God?" Quite clearly, the word of God was very conspicuous in the revivals that swept Judah and Jerusalem in the reigns of Jehoshaphat (IIChron.17:9) and Josiah. (IIKings 23:2) And here we see the same thing in the revival days of Ezra and his contemporary Nehemiah. Even the very place of their meeting may have some meaning for us. It was before the water gate, a place that could suggest to us thoughts of the refreshing and cleansing power of the word of God when applied to heart and mind.

Reading and Receiving the Word of God

Two things stand out about that Bible reading. The first was how the word was read and the second, how the word was received. It was read distinctly, and the sense was given, so that the people were able to understand the reading. Some have suggested that the thirteen men associated with Ezra in this business were there simply to translate the reading from Hebrew into Aramaic which was now the language spoken by the people. But the emphasis upon the people's understanding of the reading would seem to indicate that the actual reading was accompanied by both an interpretation and an application of the word.

Those who read the scriptures in public should labour to do so distinctly; unnecessary difficulties should not be put in the way of the hearer. And then, those charged with the task of explaining the scriptures should set forth their expositions in such a way that the least sophisticated listener will get the message. It may even have been the case that the public reading by Ezra was followed by a dispersal of the people into groups, each group being presided over by one of the thirteen who stood with him.

Certainly the profound effect of that reading upon the people is put down to the fact that "they had understood the words that were declared unto them." (v.12) The specific word translated understand in this verse carries the idea of discrimination and discernment. There was more to their understanding than a mere mental grasp of the words. In the parable of the sower our Lord taught that of all who hear the word, it is fruitful only in those who understand it. (Matt.13:23)

A further notable feature of the whole exercise was the way the word was received. When Ezra opened the book the people stood to their feet. (v.5) This indicated a healthy spirit of reverence. And then the people bowed their heads and worshipped the Lord, with their faces to the ground. (v.6) Such an attitude of reverent worship is still needed if we are to receive the word of God to the profit of our souls. We need to prepare our hearts and seek the help of the Holy Spirit as we approach God's word. There are always moral conditions required on our part if the word of God is to profit us.

Nor should we overlook the fact that the people took a great deal of time over the word, and they gave earnest attention to what they were hearing. (v.3) This is a very practical detail, and one recorded for our learning. We may not always be able to give the same time to the word as they did on that day, but then that was a special occasion for them. The principle however, is plain, we must regularly set aside time to read and study the word of God. We must not simply scan the page as we might scan the page of a newspaper, we must ponder the detail of the word as we read it, for only then will it become food for our souls.

The People's Response

When the people heard the law of God they were reminded again of the causes that lay behind the exile in Babylon. "For all the people wept, when they heard the words of the law." (v.9) In the presence of God they faced up to the gravity of the sin that had brought about the captivity. The actual reading of the law on that occasion calls to our minds the feast of Trumpets, (see Numbers 10.) and its effect upon the people reminds us of the feast of Atonement.

The principle exercise of the feast of Atonement, from a subjective point of view, was that the people were to afflict their souls. (Lev.16:31) And this is precisely the effect that the reading of the law had upon the people. It was one thing for them to sit down and weep by the rivers of Babylon, but the weeping on this occasion was the result of true repentance before God.

But Nehemiah (who may not yet have left the city or who may have simply left this instruction) and Ezra, and the Levites, said unto all the people, "This day is holy unto the Lord your God; mourn not nor weep." (v.9) Weep not, but rejoice! It may be that here we have at least a partial fulfilment of an earlier prophecy, "The ransomed of the Lord shall return, and come to Zion with songs and everlasting joy upon their heads; they shall obtain joy and gladness, and sorrow and sighing shall flee away." (Isa.35:10) We say a partial fulfilment for this pledge will surely find its full and final answer in a still future day.

The joy of the Lord was given as the reason for this exhortation. "The joy of the Lord is your strength." (v.10) It was not their joy or even their joy in the Lord, the phrase should be understood as referring to the Lord's own joy. Therein lay the secret of their strength. The Lord always delights in an obedient people. Just as their disobedience had occasioned the captivity, so now their obedience had brought joy to the heart of God and blessing and power to themselves. It is always like that. Obedience will ever bring joy to the Lord and blessing to His people. To an obedient people this word is still true, "The joy of the Lord is your strength."

That remarkable day, which began with great weeping as the causes of their calamities were brought home to them, ended with even greater rejoicing. It became an occasion of holy feasting, eating the fat and drinking the sweet. It also became a day of sharing, for portions were sent to those for whom nothing had been prepared. (v.10) All this surely represents a spiritual condition that needs to be recovered today. A group of Christians who are clearly enjoying the Lord and who are busy sharing Him with others will stand out in any company.

Meeting No 2

"On the second day were gathered together the heads of the fathers of all the people, the priests, and the Levites, unto Ezra, the scribe, to understand the words of the law." (v.13) Evidently the purpose of this assembly was to consider in more detail the word that had just been read. They had been reading in the book of Leviticus and they had come to the instructions regarding the feasts, and especially the feast of Tabernacles. (See Lev. 23.)

A superficial reading might suggest that their keeping of this feast was the first time it had been observed since the days of Joshua. (v.17) But this can hardly have been the case since we know that the feast of Tabernacles was also kept in the days of Solomon. (IIChron.8:13) The meaning seems to be that on this occasion greater attention was paid to the finer details, such an attention as had not been applied through the years, even as far back as to the days of Joshua.

This attention to detail brought to light an aspect of Tabernacles that apparently had been lost for generations. The law clearly stated that the children of Israel should dwell in booths in the feast of the seventh month. (v.14) But this practice seems to have fallen into disuse.

Back to Booths

And now, after so long a time, the people went forth and made themselves booths, every one upon the roof of his house, and in their courts, and in the courts of the house of God. etc. All the congregation sat under the booths...and there was very great gladness. (v.16,17) The Hebrew word for booth is "Succoth". These booths were temporary dwellings made from branches of trees, and sometimes used as shelters for cattle.

In picture form, the whole scene teaches us important lessons. Those temporary houses stood in contrast to their regular houses. The latter were well founded in the earth whereas the former were not. To observe this feast in the prescribed manner would surely be a reminder to the people of the transient nature of the things of this world. And it would induce in all those who were exercised in heart about what they were doing, a determination to set their affections on things eternal.

For our part, such a reminder is timely. We seem to have forgotten that this world is not our home; that we are only passing through. We have so dramatically conformed to the life styles and standards of them that dwell on the earth, we seem to have overlooked the fact that "All that is in the world, and the lust of the flesh, and the lust of the eyes and the pride of life, is not of the Father, but is of the world. And the world passes away, and the lust thereof; but he that does the will of God abides forever." (1John 2:16,17) We must constantly bring ourselves back to this basic premise that here we have no continuing city, but we seek one to come.

The Feast of Tabernacles

As for the feast itself there are some very interesting parallels to be drawn between it and the Christian's feast, the Lord's supper. Tabernacles was a feast of remembrance. (Lev.23:42,43) And as already noted, the Hebrew word for booth was succoth. This would have reminded the people of their exodus from Egypt, for when God brought them to their first encampment it was located at a place called Succoth. (Ex.12:37,13:20) Our feast too, is a feast of remembrance. We remember Him who died and rose again for our deliverance.

But Tabernacles was also a feast of thanksgiving. It was a kind of harvest home. It marked the ingathering of the fruit of the land. (Lev.23:39) At the institution of the Christian's feast the Saviour gave thanks. And when we who love Him keep the feast, we keep it as the divinely appointed expression of our corporate thanks. We should not be like the lepers who were cleansed. Only one returned to give thanks and, very significantly, as the Saviour noted, he was a Samaritan.

And then, the feast of Tabernacles was also a feast of anticipation. It was a seven day feast but it reached its climax on the eighth day. (Lev.23:39) The eighth day marked the start of a new week and points forward to the time when God will make all things new. That regeneration of all things will be brought about by the second advent of our Lord and by the events set in motion by His return. Again, Tabernacles was a yearly feast, whereas ours is a weekly anticipation of the return of our Lord from heaven. We observe our feast in the knowledge that we do so only, "Till He come."

And so the word of the Lord grew and multiplied in those days. First the word was read, then it was studied and finally it was obeyed. The people were united around the word. They were reverent, attentive, discerning and obedient. This in turn brought great joy to the heart of God and it rejoiced the hearts of His people at Jerusalem. There was very great gladness and the joy of the Lord was their strength. The foundation of blessing in our day is the same as it was then - the word that God has given to us and our subjection to it.

THE FAULT LINE

Yet another meeting of the people is detailed for us in this chapter. The purpose on this occasion was to express their sense of humiliation before the Lord and to give themselves to prayer. If the time period was a twelve hour day then three hours were given to the reading of the word of God and three hours to confessing their sins. The whole exercise followed in a natural sequence from the events of the previous chapter.

Meeting No 3

The record begins with the people separating themselves from all foreigners, that is, from people who were not within the covenant, and it ends with them, in a quite emphatic way, subjecting themselves to the authority of God's word. This throws into bold relief the difference between the two parts of this book. The first part was about the building of the wall which represents separation in an outward and legal sense but here the separation is inward and moral; true separation will always be a matter of the heart.

The Glory of God

The day began with the Levites leading the people in an act of worship, the dominant note of which was adoration. Their worship had as its very definite focus the glory of God, the Creator and the Sustainer of all things. "Blessed be thy glorious name, which is exalted above all blessing and praise. Thou, even thou, art Lord alone; thou hast made heaven, the heaven of heavens, with all their host, the earth, and all things that are in it, the seas, and all that is in them, and thou preservest them all; and the host of heaven worships you." (vv5,6) This is surely one of the most splendid doxologies anywhere on record.

Worship is the highest act of the human spirit and adoration is its essence. Indeed, it might be argued with some justification that it is only when we adopt an attitude of worship, that we are in a right condition of heart to receive impressions from the Almighty and to learn His ways. Certainly it was in this context that the Levites proceeded to address the people who had come together.

There is nothing new in what the Levites had to say, they simply reviewed the history of Israel from the call of Abram to that present time. However, after highlighting the pattern of God's dealings with His people across those years, they identified with pungent clarity a fault line that had run right through the entire period.

The Grace of God

This God of glory had acted in marvellous grace in all His dealings with His people. In grace, Abram had been called out of Mesopotamia and in grace, the nation that sprung from Abram had been redeemed from the bondage of Egypt. It was God, acting in grace, who had led and fed the people all through the long wilderness journey which ultimately brought them to Canaan. Grace had also sustained them across the intervening generations. And even when they had failed, the grace of God was manifested in their recovery. And it was that same grace that had brought these worshippers to this point in time and to this place where they were now assembled.

The prayer recorded for us here is probably only a summary of how they approached into the presence of God. They set God Himself before their hearts. They extolled Him as the God of eternity, who had made the heavens. He was also the God of history, and of overruling sovereignty. This prayer stands on the same plane as the prayers of Daniel (Dan 9) and Ezra (Ezra 9). It might also be compared with the prayer of Solomon at the dedication of the Temple. (See1Kings 8.) It is interesting to note that the pattern of this prayer is remarkably similar to those model presentations of the gospel at Jerusalem and Antioch by both Stephen and Paul respectively. (See Acts 7 & Acts 13.)

On this occasion the Levites, standing upon the stairs (i.e. the platform) remembered how God had separated Abram and how He had blessed him. (vv.7,8) Then they recalled how God had brought the children of Israel out of Egypt with great judgements (vv.9-11) and how He had led them by a cloudy pillar during the daytime, and at night by a pillar of fire, and so He gave them light for the way in which they should go. He gave them bread from heaven for their hunger; and for their thirst He brought forth water out of the rock. He also gave them a gracious pledge that He would bring them into the land which He had promised to them as their inheritance.

But the fault line already referred to soon began to open up. "Our fathers hardened their necks, and hearkened not to your commandments, and refused to obey." (vv.16,17) That was their great weakness. The painful problem of disobedience, which had first raised its head in the garden of Eden, asserted itself again and again in the history of Abraham's seed. Following their redemption from Egypt, their failure in this vital matter resulted in that whole generation being unable to enter the promised inheritance.

And why did they not enter in? The answer is concise and to the point, "They could not enter in because of unbelief." (Hebs.3:19) Quite clearly, the point of reference here is to the behaviour of the people at Kadesh-Barnea. The word from the Lord at that time was that they should go in and possess the land. A good land flowing with milk and honey. But unbelief said, let us first send spies to see if it really is a good land. It seemed that the word of man or of a few men would be more reliable than the word of God. In the event, the old spirit of rebellion re-asserted itself. They disobeyed God and they rejected His word.

Kadesh Barnea was a defining moment for that generation. It brought to light an inherent weakness. What happened at that point became a watershed. Unbelief had become so rooted in their hearts, and rebellion so entrenched, they actually considered appointing a captain who would lead them back to Egypt. Only Caleb and Joshua, who wholly followed the Lord, entered into the good of the inheritance, the rest died in the wilderness. (See Num.13.)

We forget at our peril that these things were recorded for our instruction. "Take heed, brethren, lest there be in any of you an evil heart of unbelief in departing from the living God." (Hebs.3:12) Because of the natural propensity of the carnal nature that is in us all such warnings should be carefully heeded. The really great danger for us is not that we might come short of heaven, but rather, that we might fail to realise in this present time the purpose for which God has saved us.

The Goodness of God

After them, however, another generation was raised up who did enter Canaan. For almost forty years this new generation proved the faithfulness of God. He took not away the pillar of cloud by day, nor the pillar of fire by night, so that they might know the way by which they should go. During the entire period they lacked nothing. Their clothes did not become threadbare and their shoes did not wear out. A simple statement on the page of inspiration says it all, "Their feet swelled not." (v.21)

He led them from victory to victory and He multiplied their seed so that they possessed the gate of their enemies. Under the leadership of Joshua, and at a time when the Jordan overflowed its banks, they

crossed the river as on dry land. In Canaan itself, they first engaged
and then subdued the resident nations, and in the course of three
brilliantly fought campaigns they won many notable victories. It
was the Lord's doing and marvellous in their eyes.

It was the Lord who gave those nations into their hands. Moreover,
the gift was in good measure, pressed down and running over. For
this all took place at a season of the year when they found themselves
in possession of well stocked cities and a fat land, full of all good
things. Where others had laboured, they entered into their labours.
And so they ate of the fat of the land and rejoiced in the goodness of
their God. (v.24,25)

Nevertheless, they too proved no better than their fathers. They
were disobedient and rebellious. In course of time they cast away
the law of the Lord, they slew His prophets and provoked Him to
anger. God had powerfully used them as a scourge to judge those
Canaanite nations for their evil deeds, just as He had pledged to do
four hundred years earlier in the covenant He made at that time with
Abraham. (See Genesis 15.) But now, He turned the tables and used
those same nations as a scourge to judge His people, that in this way
He might bring them back again to Himself. (v.27)

Judges Kings Prophets

And when they repented and called upon the Lord, He heard their
cry and delivered them. He raised up Judges who were saviours and
deliverers of the people. But time and again, their repentance proved
like the morning cloud for when a given judge died they would show
themselves still a rebellious people, they would turn yet again from
following the Lord. Departure followed by discipline was the
constantly repeated pattern. Then there would come a season of
gracious deliverance, but it was only for a few short years, to be
followed by yet another apostasy.

But the patience of God was very wonderful. He sent Prophets to
His people. And through them the Spirit bore powerful witness and

testified against their sins. Alas, their pride, their stubbornness and their rebellion would not allow them to hear the voice of God through the prophets. And they became hardened through the deceitfulness of sin. But although they deserved His judgement, God still dealt with them in marvellous grace and in tender mercy.

After the Judges (v.27) and the Prophets (v.30) God raised up Kings (v.32) for the people. The first king was Saul. But God's thoughts were not with Saul (he was the people's choice) God's thoughts were with David. He was the sweet psalmist of Israel and the man after God's own heart. Then after him came Solomon. But warning was given even in those heady days of David and Solomon that departure from the Lord would be followed by judgement. Alas, departure was already in evidence in Solomon's old age. And after his death, the kingdom was divided under Rehoboam. The ten northern tribes became disconnected from the two southern tribes and, to this day, the two parts have never been reunited.

The story of the ten northern tribes, known now as Israel, was one dark and lamentable tale until they were eventually carried away by the king of Assyria. (See 2Kings17:4.) The history of the two southern tribes, commonly called Judah, was only just a little better. And finally, in the days of Zedekiah, who was the last of a long line of kings to sit upon the throne of David and Solomon at Jerusalem, the seventy year captivity in Babylon took place. But now the return from that captivity had been so recent and the circumstances of it so fresh in their minds, these worshippers could easily discern that the goodness of God to them in their day, was equal to that same goodness in the days of their fathers.

They Justified God

But if the goodness of God was such, why had all this evil befallen His people? The reason was always the same, now as of old. Neither the kings, nor the princes, nor the priests, nor the fathers, kept God's law or hearkened to His commandments. And it was only through His abundant mercy that these worshippers had been brought to the place where they now stood on the twenty fourth day of that seventh month.

Having traced the fault line through the years and having acknowledged their waywardness, the Levites now led the people to do something that must have had great meaning for them. They frankly and openly justified God and, of course, in doing so they condemned themselves. They said, "you are just in all that is brought upon us; for you have done right, but we have done wickedly." (v.33) In this they stood in contrast to the Pharisees of our Lord's time whose first line of defence was always to justify themselves.

Jesus said, "Wisdom is justified of all her children." (Luke 7:35) Experience seems to prove that this is still the case. A distinguishing feature of all who are truly the Lord's is that they are ready to judge themselves and, in the process, to justify God. In this they stand apart, and are in marked contrast to others who reject the counsel of God just as the Pharisees rejected it. (See Luke 7:29,30.)

But the work of that memorable day was not yet complete. Before the sun went down a decision was taken to draw up a solemn covenant in which the people bound themselves under oath to maintain the integrity of their commitment to the Lord. A list of those who sealed the covenant and the precise terms of the covenant itself are found in the next chapter. And here again we shall find that the details of these ancient records speak powerfully to us and to our generation.

THE SOLEMN LEAGUE AND COVENANT

The covenant referred to at the close of the last chapter is recorded in some detail in the chapter now before us. To begin with, we have the names of the heads of the families who sealed the covenant. Together they formed what was known among the Jews, as the great synagogue. Originally, the great synagogue had one hundred and twenty members but this figure was later reduced to seventy. This supreme council of the Jewish people was known simply as the Sanhedrin in our Lord's time.

As a whole, believers in this dispensation do not consider themselves a covenantal people. This basic premise leads to a certain reserve in matters such as the issuing of decision cards which were very popular some time ago. For the same reason we do not require people to sign pledges of loyalty and we regard with some suspicion, the whole idea of calling upon people to make New Year resolutions etc.

Our attitude to these things flows, as much from our experience as it does from the absence of any New Testament precedent. Such covenants are often made in the energy of the flesh and that can only fail. In addition, the scriptures clearly teach that it is better not to vow, than to vow and not pay. But the main reason for our position is the nature of Christianity itself.

Because of the essentially spiritual nature of Christianity, if some believer should be burdened in his heart to make a covenant of any kind, he should do so between himself and the Lord. He should make his vow in the secret place before God, and he should do so, mindful of the fact that it is to the Lord he must one day give account.

A reading of church history will show that many honoured servants of God, through deep searchings of heart, came to a place where they gave themselves to the Lord in this way. That their act of dedication had about it the appearance of a covenant between themselves and the Lord is beyond all doubt. But such strivings were personal to themselves and not something to be arbitrarily imposed upon others.

Israel - A Covenant People

The solemn league and covenant of our chapter, however, was in perfect accord with the nature of Judaism, for in contrast to the Church, Israel was a covenantal people. Judaism was established upon the great covenants of God. There was the Abrahamic covenant (see Gen.15.) and the two Mosaic covenants, one at the beginning and the other at the end, of the wilderness journey. And after that, there was the Davidic covenant, in which God promised to David a seed and a house and a throne forever. (See II Sam.7.)

And then, of course, there is the new covenant. Quite plainly it too has national connotations. "I will make a new covenant with the house of Israel and with the house of Judah." (Jer.31:31-34) At the same time it is clear that others will share in the benefits of the new covenant. We know that the Gentiles are to receive blessing under the terms of the Abrahamic covenant even though that covenant was made with Abraham personally and with his seed. In the same way, the new covenant in Jesus' blood is the basis on which God is saving the Church in this age and on which He will save Israel in the age to come.

Commitment

But the covenant we are considering was different from all those covenants in that it was initiated by the people themselves. And in making it they were assuming, under oath, certain obligations that would be binding upon themselves and their offspring. The thing that should really concern us is the principle lying behind the making of covenants, the principle of a binding commitment to certain agreed obligations. Parallels might be drawn between this solemn league and the covenant of marriage, which has at its very core the idea of commitment. The marriage ceremony, with its vows and pledges, its witnesses and its signings, clearly spells out the commitment of one partner to the other.

To many, all this emphasis upon commitment in marriage is considered old hat for in our day the preference seems to be for a couple simply to live together without the trouble of being married at all. It is called cohabitation. The absence of any mutual or formal commitment has the advantage, so it is argued, that if there does come a parting of the ways, the separation will be simplicity itself. In reality, the far reaching and painful consequences of such an arrangement, when it breaks down, are regularly documented in all the newspapers for everyone to see.

Marriage, above all else, is a loving relationship and where there is true love, it will always involve commitment. Marriage by its very nature requires an open and public commitment on the part of the bride and the groom to each other. This is in keeping with the scriptures which teach that Christ loved the church and gave Himself for it. The supreme lover is our supreme pattern. Even He could not have done more to demonstrate His commitment, because He gave

Himself. For our part, by joining our hearts with His, we declare our love for Him and our commitment to do His will.

The Signatories and their Pledges

As we have already noted, this chapter begins with a list of those who sealed the covenant. We would say, they put their signatures to it. It then sets forth their resolve to walk in God's Law, (v.29) and their determination not to forsake God's House (v.39). Evidently a penalty was to be applied in the event of the covenant being broken for there was a curse attached to it as well as an oath (v.29).

The people's resolve, as it was enshrined in the covenant, specified three things. First, there was the keeping of God's law, with special reference to the question of marriage. Then there was God's day and finally there was the matter of maintaining God's house. Each of these things had been matters of repeated failure in their history. That very failure contributed to, and eventually reached its climax in, the Babylonian exile. Alas, after a few short years all three covenant issues were being compromised once more by the people of Jerusalem. Significantly, in our own day these same three things are again matters of grave concern to those who seek to maintain the testimony of our Lord.

God's Law

The primary issue in that day was the people's attitude to the Law of God. Of course, this always is the central issue of faith. It was so in the days of Zerubbabel and those who came with him from Babylon. Ezra too, and his companions found this to be the key issue of their time. And so it has been throughout this present age. The issue above all other issues at the time of the protestant reformation was Sola Scriptura, scripture alone. And in the ongoing experience of the Christian church the matter of first importance has always been the place that should be given to the word of God.

This primary issue impinged upon the lives of the people in an exceedingly practical sense. It raised the whole question of separation in marriage. "We will not give our daughters unto the people of the land, nor take their daughters for our sons." (v.30) Provision had always been in place for an Israelite to marry outside the Hebrew race. But this was permissible only after the outsider had first come among God's people and had given evidence that he or she had embraced Israel's God. A notable example of this was Ruth who married Boaz. She confessed to Naomi, her mother- in-law by a previous marriage, "Your people shall be my people, and your God my God." (Ruth1:16)

In any other circumstance, such marriages ran the very real risk that the persons concerned would bring in their gods among the covenant people and thus in one form or another, and perhaps almost by stealth, idolatory would be introduced. This was plainly not acceptable. The prohibition therefore, was not a simple matter of racial prejudice for, quite plainly, a mixed marriage raised a host of questions which were profoundly spiritual and religious.

The outstanding example of this in the nation's history was Solomon. He married many foreign women who turned away his heart from following the Lord. (See 1Kings 11:1.) Over the years, the lesson of Solomon had been forgotten but now it was to be enshrined as a vital part of this solemn league and covenant.

While there are many factors that establish compatibility within marriage, the marriage of a believer and an unbeliever clearly constitutes an unequal yoke and is a violation of what God has enjoined upon His people. The scriptures could hardly be more explicit on this matter, "Be not unequally yoked together with unbelievers." (2Cor.6:14) This principle needs to be stressed in a day when the frontiers of light and darkness are being increasingly blurred.

The mighty David who, we have already noted, was the sweet psalmist of Israel, the man after God's own heart, failed at this very point and reaped a terrible harvest. He married a pagan woman who came from Geshur. (See IISam.3:3.) She became the mother of

Absalom who wrought such mischief for David, both in his family and in the wider circle of his kingdom.

Failure at this point has led to much compromise and caused many problems, especially where children have been involved. When difficulties arise in such a context, as difficulties will arise even in the best ordered homes, the children often find themselves torn between the opposing parties and pulled in opposite directions. The unequal yoke has occasioned much sorrow, not only in family circles, but also in many fellowships of believers where it may have been carelessly tolerated.

God's Day

Another matter upon which they covenanted together was the integrity of the sabbath day (v.31). At the dawn of creation God had established the principle of one day in seven as a day of rest. "On the seventh day God ended His work which He had made; and He rested on the seventh day from all His work. And God blessed the seventh day, and sanctified it, because that in it He had rested from all His work." (Gen.2:2,3) Following the exodus from Egypt God gave the sabbath to Israel as a sign of the special covenant relationship that existed between Himself and the nation. (See Ex.31:12-17.)

In the first instance, therefore, the observance of one day in seven as a day of rest has a humanitarian base. It is fairly generally recognised that the human species needs one day in seven as a diversion from its normal toil. But the fact that the day identified to be that day of rest, was the seventh day, testified to God as the creator of all. For in six days the Lord made heaven and earth, and rested on the seventh day. And so the observance of the sabbath day carried certain spiritual overtones beyond its purely benefical effect upon the health of the human race.

The Christian's day of rest is the first day of the week, and it too is observed as a memorial, a memorial of the new creation. On the first day of the week Jesus rose from the dead to become the head of an entirely new order. Following that, almost every significant development in the life of the early church took place on the first day of the week. The appearances of the risen Lord to His own and the outpouring of the Holy Spirit are notable examples. The first day of the week was also the time when the Lord's Supper was observed and on that same day the disciples were exhorted to bring their offerings.(1Cor.16:2)

And so whatever material or physical advantage attached to it, Israel's observance of the sabbath became a witness to the surrounding nations that they were different. An Israelite closing his stall on the sabbath was declaring that he belonged to a people in covenant relationship with Jehovah. The nation's observance of that day was a simple and graphic way of bearing testimony to who they were and to whom they belonged. And so they covenanted that if the people of the land brought goods to sell on the sabbath day, they would not buy from them on that day. (v.31)

In the same way we can bear a similar telling witness by our regard for the Lord's day. Just as Israel found herself among hostile nations so we are in the presence of a hostile world. Just as for them the keeping of the sabbath as a day apart was a witness to others, so our approach to the first day can be a singular testimony to our ungodly neighbours. And like the Israelites, we who are Christians find that this witness does not even require us to open our mouths.

The sabbath was hedged about with rules which governed its observance. No such hedge is put around the Lord's day and this is in keeping with the new dispensation. However, we can learn much about how we should behave on the Lord's day by considering the activities of the risen Lord Himself on that day, throughout the period between His resurrection and His ascension. Furthermore, what the early believers did on the first day of the week presents us with added guidance as to how we should observe the Lord's day.

We are convinced that if a Christian businessman has a conviction that he should not trade on the first day of the week, God will surely honour him for being true to that conviction, and the rest of us should not set ourselves up as judges or juries. The pattern of our Lord and His apostles would teach us that the day should be spent in the worship and service of God and in meeting with His people. It should be different from the other days.

But not only had Israel been given the sabbath day, they were also given the sabbath year. And it too, was a very important ordinance. It raised environmental or green issues. The land needed rest as well as the people and if it was treated with care, it would, in turn, serve its people well. The keeping of the seventh year meant no plowing, sowing or reaping, and its observance was intended as a sign of Israel's faith in God. Could they trust God to supply their needs for a whole year?

During the sabbath year the collection of debts would not be pressed (v.31). Not only the land but also the poor, and especially any who had contracted debts, were to have a season of respite. The debt may not have been cancelled but, at least for that year, it lay dormant. God would teach His people the value of love and compassion. In all these provisions we can discern a beautiful harmony between a healthy regard for God's creation and the integrity of a people's life and witness.

But Israel failed to honour the Lord in this important matter. The seventh year sabbath had been neglected for an extended period of 490 years. Seventy such sabbaths had come and gone without observance. It was this that determined the length of the captivity in Babylon. It lasted precisely seventy years so that the land might enjoy her sabbaths. (See IIChron.36:21.) The weekly sabbath seems to have fared little better, for its desecration was among the many charges levelled against the nation by Isaiah the prophet. (See Isa.58:13.)

God's House

And then, the third covenant issue concerned the provision of all that was necessary for the service and maintenance of the House of

God, (v.32) for the support of the Priests (v.36) and for the Levites. (v.37) A footnote to the covenant said, "We will not forsake the house of our God." (v.39) The word used means that they would not fail to provide for the house of God. Their determination in this matter involved some very far reaching and intensely practical commitments.

The law required the payment of a half shekel but they charged themselves with the payment of an additional one third of a shekel to maintain the house (v.32). This meant that their giving had about it the quality of sacrifice. Moreover, their giving was systematic for they made provision for the Temple services and for all the offerings and for the special needs of the many special occasions (v.33).

They also cast lots for the bringing of the wood offering (v.34). This probably related to the Mosaic requirement that the fire on the altar should never go out. Keeping the fire burning required a constant supply of wood and so an arrangement was made by lots to cover this need. (See Lev.6.)

But above all, every man pledged to do his best for the house of God. This is seen in the emphasis placed upon the giving of the firstfruits unto the Lord. (Neh.10:35-37) The mention of the firstfruits would always remind a godly Jew of the redemption from Egypt. Thereafter, God claimed the firstborn of man and of beast and when they came into the land, the firstfruits of the ground were His as well. Redemption, therefore, was the inspiration of that solemn league and covenant as it must be the inspiration of all true service. "We love Him because He first loved us." (1John 4:19)

The principle of tithing was also enshrined in the covenant. This was necessary for the maintenance of the personnel involved in the ministry of the house. Besides the priests, there were the Levites and the porters and the singers. These all had to be provided for, and the returned exiles were not insensitive to their needs. A timeless yardstick by which we can judge any group of people claiming to be the Lord's, is their treatment of the Lord's servants who are among them. (See Matt.23:34,35.)

It is true that of all the matters dealt with in the covenant, the house of God comes last. But this must not be thought of as minimising its significance. Nehemiah knew the value of worship to the health of the nation. The importance of the house of God was that it represented Israel as a worshipping people. However much it might be argued that we cannot enrich God, even by our worship, the fact remains that if we cease to worship, we will seriously impoverish ourselves. A people who have ceased to worship very soon show signs of moral breakdown and decay. May we never cease to be true worshippers, who worship the Father in Spirit and in truth.

EverY MaN In HiS PlacE

The wall having been built, and to that extent the city secured, it now had to be defended. This required the establishment of a garrison within its precincts and the introducton of some sort of order among the people. Numerically they were greatly outnumbered, consequently wisdom demanded that a strategic use should be made of all available personnel. And so this new chapter details for us who dwelt where and for what reason.

Not surprisingly, this chapter is another list of names. But also included are many details and insights that will reward careful study. It is scarcely necessary to note that the people whose names appear could hardly have imagined that two and a half millennia later their names and their service would still be spoken of. The message is as plain as it is powerful, any service done for the Lord, however insignificant in man's eyes, will not be forgotten. It will have its reward.

The placing of the people in their various locations reminds us that God is a God of order. "God is not the author of confusion."(1Cor.14:33) This principle seems to be implicit throughout the scriptures. Take creation week as an example, if we attempted to switch the work of the second and fifth days, we would plainly make a nonsense of the beautiful and sequential order of the six workdays of God. Or again, when Israel went out of Egypt it is recorded that they went up harnessed. (Ex.13:18) Some scholars say the word means, marshalled in ranks of fives. The record certainly implies that they marched out as an ordered company and not like an undisciplined rabble. In the Tabernacle in the wilderness as well as in the Temple in the land we also find both order and organisation.

The church at Colosse seems to have had a reputation for godly order. Paul wrote approvingly to them, "I am with you in spirit, joying and beholding your order, and the steadfastness of your faith in Christ." (Col.2:5) And here in Jerusalem after the signing of the solemn league and covenant there was a similar arranging of the people into an orderly community. All this required a large degree of discipline, and above all a predisposition to accept personal restraint and a readiness to endure the inconvenient.

Where shall we live

About fifty thousand people had returned from Babylon, but not all dwelt at Jerusalem. (vv.1,4,6) Some dwelt in the cities of Judah, and others inhabited the villages. (vv.20,25) However, Jerusalem was the focal point of the people's interest and therefore special attention was given to have it adequately serviced. At the same time Jerusalem was the focus of the enemy's interest. This meant that the city which is now for the first time called the holy city, was not a much sought after or desirable place of residence. Even to-day people like to distance themselves from areas of terrorist activity.

What they decided was this, the rulers or princes would dwell in Jerusalem and then lots were to be cast to bring every tenth person to dwell within the city. It was just then that certain men stepped foward and willingly offered themselves to dwell there. The rest of the people, deeply moved by the courage and self sacrifice of these men, were unstinting in their admiration. We read that, "The people blessed all the men, who willingly offered themselves to dwell at Jerusalem." (v.2)

Not by constraint, but willingly; not for filthy lucre, but of a ready mind, was how Peter exhorted the elders to do their work. (1Pet.5:2) The willing or ready mind is still basic to all true Christian service. When Moses was launched upon the great task of building a house for God in the wilderness, he was surrounded by a willing hearted people. All that was needed for the task was supplied by the freewill offerings of the people themselves. Everyone had a contribution to make, but there was neither force nor coercion, all was entirely voluntary, and all the need was met. The men of Jerusalem, like the people of Moses' day teach us that of all we may do or give in the service of Christ, it is the service rendered by those whose hearts have been made willing by the constraining influence of the love of Christ that will have His approval.

Gift and Grace

This ordering of the people covered the entire range of the various tasks that had to be undertaken. And in turn, therefore, it had to take into account the gifts and abilities of those who would be involved. In Christian service the same conditions apply. "Unto every one of us is given grace according to the measure of the gift of Christ." (Eph.4:7) At Jerusalem, there appears to have been a remarkable identity between the variety of gift available and the diversity of the need.

The constant conflict with the enemy called forward men of valour. "All the sons of Perez...were valiant men." (v.6) The brethren of Amashai were mighty men of valour, and their overseer was Zabdiel, the son of one of the great men (v.14). The former were soldiers while the latter were priests and their nearness to the Lord only seems to have increased their might. Such men are still required.

Men whose aim it is to be strong, not in their own strength, but in the grace that is in Christ Jesus. (2Tim.2:1)

There were others who led the praise. A decendant of Asaph was their appointed leader. It would appear that his primary task was to introduce the prayer times with seasons of praise (v.17). We could profitably take a leaf out of his book. Our prayer meetings are often devoid of any real expressions of meaningful praise. The prevailing tendency seems to be to approach the throne of grace almost as beggars who have forgotten past mercies. We should count our blessings and name them one by one, for it is important to itemise our thanksgivings. (See Psa.107.) We must constantly stir up our souls to praise the Lord, and we should ever be mindful of His benefits.

Then there were the porters who had the charge of the gates. They were the front line men so far as the security of the city was concerned. Earlier we noted the vitally important role of the gatekeepers when the wall was just finished. (See Neh.7:3.) Their task was no less important now. These men had to observe times, sunrise and sunset. They had to guard that none would enter the city by climbing in some other way. The admission of the wrong people into the holy city could have far reaching consequences.

Attention is called to the business of the house of God, and a noteworthy distinction was drawn between the outward and the inward business of the house. (Compare vv.16&22.) Christianity too, has about it both an outward and an inward side. At times we have majored on the former to the neglect of the latter; but the two need to be balanced. If the heart is right then surely the outward demeanour will be right as well. On the other hand it will hardly do to profess an inward experience and allow the outward manner of life to be a contradiction of that profession. The apostle James aptly and simply stated the necessary balance when he said, "I will show you my faith by my works." (Jas.2:18)

And then there were those who exercised a necessary oversight at Jerusalem. Shabbethai and Jozabad had the oversight of the outward business of the house (v.16), while Uzzi was the overseer of the Levites (v.22). This also must have some spiritual significance pertinent to the question of order among God's people to-day. What damage has been done to the testimony by men in positions of oversight who have neither the aptitude nor the spiritual equipment for such a position.

It is a solemn duty for anyone to assume oversight of God's people. Such have a heavy charge laid upon them. They must to be able to bring God's word to bear upon situations as they arise, and they must watch over the souls of their people as those who shall give account. In return, believers should remember them who have the rule over them and be ready to obey them in the Lord. (See Hebs.13:7&17.)

The singers might have thought their service not very significant. But they were provided for in a rather special way. Their maintenance was supplied on a daily basis directly by the decree of the king (v.23). This was just another instance of the king's heart being in the hand of the Lord. If we should feel that our lives are lived in comparative obscurity and our service is of little significance in the great scheme of things, let us take heart from the experience of the singers.

A Present Message

Although these events happened so long ago they have obvious lessons for the church of to-day. The great truth that Christ is risen and ascended and that the Holy Spirit is here proves that there is work to be done for the Lord. Moreover, for that work gifts have been given to the church, gifts that are to be used for the benefit of the whole body of Christ. "When He ascended up on high, He led captivity captive, and gave gifts unto men. He gave some, apostles; and some, prophets; and some, evangelists; and some, pastors and teachers; for the perfecting of the saints, for the work of the ministry, for the edifying of the body of Christ." (Eph.4:8,11,12)

In addition to these major gifts, the gifts of the Spirit were imparted to individual believers. While some of these gifts were temporary, others are permanent. The striking thing about the gifts of the Spirit is their great diversity. "For to one is given, by the Spirit, the word of wisdom; to another, the word of knowledge by the same Spirit." (1Cor.12:8) And yet, the integrity of the body as a whole, is the single all embracing purpose lying behind those gifts or manifestations of the Spirit's presence.

This places enormous responsibility on each of us who are the Lord's. By seizing opportunities for service we will stir up the gift of God that is in us. We must learn from the returned exiles and we must cultivate the gifts of the risen Lord and of the Holy Spirit that they might be exercised in a responsibile way for the furtherance of the gospel and the upbuilding of the body of Christ. The organisation of those who returned to Jerusalem is a vibrant illustration of the functioning of the gifts and abilities that God has given to His people.

Nehemiah chapter twelve

ThE DedicatioN Of ThE WalL

The opening verses of this new chapter give a list of the priests and the Levites who returned from Babylon under Zerubbabel. The high priest at that time was Joshua, and those named with him were the chiefs of the priests and of their brethren (v.7). We also have a record of the descendants of Joshua himself (vv.10,11). After that there is a list of the heads of the priests' houses in the days of Joiakim the son of Joshua (vv.12-21). And finally, the heads of the houses of the Levites are also listed (vv.22-26).

Special mention should be made of Jaddua who did not assume the office of high priest until long after Nehemiah had passed from this scene (v.22). His name was probably added to the list at a later date in order to preserve the line of descent. The importance of these registers will at once be evident if we keep in mind that from the time of the captivity to the advent of Messiah, Jewish chronology was reckoned, not by the reigns of kings and their successors, but by the various high priests and their successors.

While a detailed study of these names is sure to reap a rich reward, it is with the second part of the chapter we shall concern ourselves. The wall had been built in troublous times as foreseen by the prophet Daniel. (Dan.9:25) Now it had to be dedicated. This exercise was very important because it symbolised the end in view, the purpose, the goal for which the wall had been built. In this act of dedication the builders were proclaiming that all the labours they had engaged in had not been done for their own glory but for the glory of their God.

Dedication

Jerusalem was the city of God. It was the place where God had chosen to put His name. Every detail of the dedication of the wall, therefore, seemed to echo the words of the Psalmist, "Not unto us, O Lord, not unto us, but unto your name give glory." (Psa.115:1) We can dedicate only what belongs to us and when we dedicate anything to the Lord we are solemnly declaring our intention henceforth to hold that thing for His glory. Needless to say, it is always better not to dedicate, than to dedicate and not deliver.

The precise date of the dedication is uncertain. The generally accepted view is that it took place within a few months of the wall being completed. But some think it was later, and should be linked to the next chapter and to Nehemiah's return to Jerusalem. If that is so, then the last two chapters should be read as one and the dedication seen as a series of connected events. The matter does not seem to be of great importance and, in any case, there does appear to be compelling reasons for the earlier date. (See comments on Ch.13.)

Among the first references in scripture to dedication is one that relates to soldiers going forth to battle with the armies of Israel. The officers laid down certain conditions which had to be fulfilled, conditions which seem strange to us until we learn their spiritual significance. For instance, if a man had built a new house but had not yet dedicated it, he was disqualified from entering the army (Deut.20:5). The reason for this disqualification seems to be that only when the house was dedicated did it become a part of the wider inheritance. And only then was he free to enlist, for now he would fight, not simply to maintain his own self interest but to secure the integrity of the total inheritance.

Dedication is an act of worship, and worship is the highest and noblest exercise of which the spirit of man is capable. True worship is ascribing worthship to the object of our worship. To worship God is to recognise His supreme worthship, "For of Him, and through Him, and to Him, are all things; to whom be glory forever. Amen. (Rom.11:36) All this is cogently illustrated in the dedication of the newly built wall of Jerusalem. Every detail of that day's activity breathes the vital air of corporate worship.

We should note that before anything else was done "the priests and the Levites purified themselves, and purified the people, and the gates, and the wall." (v.30) This emphasis upon purification was a timely reminder to them of the holiness of their God. The very heavens are unclean in His sight; He does not trifle with sin. Under the old scheme of things the Jews had their preparation for the Sabbath, and we should have our preparation for the Lord's day. And of course, what obtains for corporate worship will also hold good for private worship. We always need to have prepared hearts when we seek the Lord.

Each succeeding generation of believers has asked the question, "Lord, who shall abide in your tabernacle? Who shall dwell in your holy hill?" And the answer has always been the same. "He that walks uprightly, and works righteousness, and speaks the truth in his heart." (Psa.15:1,2) In another place the Psalmist enquired, "Who shall ascend into the hill of the Lord? or who shall stand in His holy place?" These were rhetorical questions to which the questioner supplied his own answers. "He that has clean hands, and a pure heart; who has not lifted up his soul unto vanity, nor sworn deceitfully." (Psa.24:3,4) A later reference states a fact which we all need to take on board; "If I regard iniquity in my heart, the Lord will not hear me." (Psa.66:18)

On the other hand, the apostle John had a good deal to say about having confidence before God. "This is the confidence that we have in Him, that, if we ask anything according to His will, He hears us." (1John5:14) But then he qualified this, for he said, "Beloved, if our heart condemn us not, then have we confidence toward God." (1John 3:21) In the end, however, the key to confidence before God is to abide in Christ.

Let the apostle John speak again, "And now, little children, abide in Him; that, when He shall appear, we may have confidence, and not be ashamed before Him at His coming." (1John2:28) We need regularly to purify ourselves, taking account of anything that mars communion with the Lord, otherwise our worship will be unacceptable, and our pious professions, no more than sounding brass or tinkling cymbals.

Decently and in Order

The worship of the returned exiles on that day of dedication followed a definite plan, it was not in any way disorganised. The total assembly was divided into two. One company marched anti-clockwise on the wall while the other company marched clockwise. Eventually the two companies met just opposite the house of God. This might suggest the thought of unity in diversity, and of diversity in unity, which is something Paul argued strongly for in his letters, especially in his letter to the Corinthians. (See 1Cor.12:4,12) Diversity of itself should never become a ground for division for then we are all impoverised.

There was great diversity among Nehemiah's people. The Levites were sought out of all their places and brought to Jerusalem. The sons of the singers, who had built themselves villages round about Jerusalem, gathered themselves together. The princes were brought up upon the wall and the rulers were also assembled. Instead of attributing sanctity to a dull uniformity, we need to recognise the rich diversity that is found among them who call upon the name of our Lord Jesus Christ. On the occasion before us the musical instruments that were used were also many and diverse. In addition to the trumpets   there were cymbals, psalteries, and harps. (vv.27,35,41)

And yet a very beautiful order prevailed. Quite clearly, they did not slavishly follow the traditions of their fathers, but neither did they cast them aside. They learned from their past and did not forget the patterns that were preserved for them in their scriptures. "Both the singers and the porters kept the ward of their God...according to the commandment of David, and of Solomon his son. For in the days of David and Asaph of old there were chief of the singers, and songs of praise and thanksgiving unto God." (vv.45,46) Let all things be done decently and in order, urged Paul, for in this way you will both impress and influence outsiders when they come in among you. (1Cor.14:23,40)

Before the Temple, the combined choirs sang their praises, and at the same time the priests within, offered their sacrifices. It must have been a truly memorable occasion for all who were present. Each person must have carried away his own memory of the day, just as we should be able to carry away some hallowed memory of our meeting with the Lord in the company of His people. Everyone must have been impressed with the enthusiam of the occasion. Not only did the singers sing, but they sang loud (v.42). God had made them to rejoice with great joy and the involvement of the women and children surely contributed to make the joy of that day to be heard afar off. And even the sacrifices that were offered were said to have been great sacrifices (v.43). These people were wholehearted in their worship.

Nor one jarring note is recorded. In fact, not only did the choirs follow the arrangement that had been appointed for them, but other appointments were made and kept as well. The people with willing minds filled their hands with service for the Lord. Some were appointed to take charge of the storehouses; to look after the offerings and the firstfruits and the tithes. One of their primary duties was to ensure that the portions assigned by the law for the priests and the Levites actually were delivered. In that day the priests and the Levites were held in proper honour among the people.

The Giving of Thanks

But one overriding feature of the occasion was the emphasis placed upon thanksgiving. We read of some who were over the thanksgiving and of others who supported their brethren, to praise, and to give thanks, according to the commandment of David the man of God (vv.8,24). The dedication itself was kept with gladness, both with thanksgivings, and with singing (v.27). The two choirs had one common task, namely, to give thanks; and when they eventually merged into one, it was to give thanks in the house of God (vv.31,38,40). And all was done in the tradition of David and Asaph in whose day singers had been appointed to lead the songs of praise and thanksgiving unto God (v.46).

This is a feature that seems to have very largely dropped out of modern worship. Apart from an occasional cliche very little notice is taken of the debt of love we owe. With repeated emphasis we might recall again that when ten lepers were cleansed only one returned to give thanks, and he was a Samaritan. When the Lord asked, "Where are the nine?" He was calling attention to a circumstance that is recurrent in our generation. Let us remember that "It is a good thing to give thanks unto the Lord, and to sing praises unto thy name, O most High: to show forth your lovingkindness in the morning, and your faithfulness every night." (Psa.92:1,2)

These then are some of the things we can learn from the dedication of the wall. The people of God are a worshipping people. We worship the Father in Spirit and in truth, and an integral part of that worship is praise and thanksgiving. The returned exiles had their choirs and their marches and their musical instruments but what is important for us is that we should look at the principles lying behind the activities of that day of dedication and learn from them. We do not follow the forms but we must learn the disciplines that lay behind them. On that day of dedication, the people, though small in number, were confronted with the deepest and most inclusive truth of their national existence, namely, the truth of their relationship with God.

Nehemiah Returns
To Jerusalem

We know that after the building of the wall Nehemiah went back to Persia, and now this final chapter recounts the events that followed upon his return to Jerusalem. How long he was absent is uncertain, but one thing is clear, the man who returned was not one whit different from the man who had gone away. He was still possessed of the same holy zeal as at the beginning. At the same time, the situation that confronted him, upon his return, is a remarkable witness to the weakness and vanity of flesh in the things of God.

The opening phrase, "On that day," refers to the day now about to be described, the day of Nehemiah's return to Jerusalem, rather than to the dedication day of the previous chapter. In fact, this chapter seems to be yet another of those instances, often found in scripture, where the conclusion is stated first and then how the conclusion was arrived at is discussed in some detail. The case of Eliashib the priest (v.4), seems to support this view for quite clearly it pre-dates the general statement of the opening verses. In addition, the Levites were fully supported on the day of dedication but here this was not the case (v.10).

Nehemiah upon his return to Jerusalem was faced with all the evidences of a profound decline in the spiritual life of the remnant. With some justification he might have expected to have found it otherwise. Following the building of the wall great reforms had been introduced and with great ceremony the covenant had been signed; solemn commitments had been entered into, and then, after all that, there was the great act of dedication.

We cannot doubt the sincerity of those loud professions of the previous chapters, but evidently there was not the moral energy to carry those professions through to reality, certainly not in any permanent way. It seems that by the time of Nehemiah's return every issue included in the covenant had been compromised. Well did Jesus say, "the flesh profiteth nothing." (John 6:63)

But the final chapter details the vigour and courage with which Nehemiah addressed the failure and how he laboured to recover the situation. That he had good success only proves his own strength of character because a few years down the line, Malachi, the last of the prophets, recorded the deplorable condition of the people who had departed yet again from God and His word. Their repentance had been like the morning cloud.

The Word - Read and Obeyed

The practice of publicly reading the law of Moses, initiated by Ezra (Neh.8:1), might have been discontinued while Nehemiah was absent from Jerusalem. But even if that was not the case, there certainly was an open and flagrant disobedience of the law. On the day in question, they read in the book of Deuteronomy, "That the Ammonite and the Moabite should not come into the congregation of God forever." (Deut.23:3) This prohibition had been introduced after those nations had failed to facilitate, with bread and water, the passage of the children of Israel through the wilderness; and because they had hired Baalim the false prophet, to curse Israel. In the event, God turned the curse into a blessing.

That particular piece of their history, with all its significance for the people, both historical and practical, they had simply set aside and mixed multitude conditions had been allowed to develop at Jerusalem. It is not enough to read God's word, we must obey it. On that day, probably under the influence of Nehemiah, the people acted upon what was written and "they separated from Israel all the mixed multitude." (v.3) The incident serves to highlight a reality that has been proved over and over again, namely, that a basic cause of weakness among the people of God is a neglect of His precious word.

It was disobedience to the clearly revealed will of God that robbed our first parents of paradise; and the generation that had been rescued from Egypt, of Canaan. The same cause had the effect of depriving king Saul of his throne. And we should never forget what Samuel said to Saul, "To obey is better than sacrifice, and to hearken than the fat of rams. For rebellion is as the sin of witchcraft, and stubbornness is as iniquity and idolatory." (1Sam.15:22,23) The words of the Lord's mother at the marriage feast have an abiding significance, "Whatsoever He says unto you, do it." (John 2:5)

The chapter before us demonstrates the recurring theme of scripture, that when the word of God is neglected all sorts of evils are set in train. Besides the matter already referred to, Nehemiah had four quite specific areas of difficulty to deal with. And we should not ignore the fact that there is a certain consequential order about these things. For instance, the first issue affected the integrity of the temple, the house of God, and the final issue affected the family life of the nation. In our own day it is impossible not to observe a similar link between these two issues.

The House of God

The first issue then, concerned the temple. While the wall was being built, Nehemiah had experienced repeated and unrelenting opposition from Sanballat and Tobiah. Imagine his astonishment when he discovered that during the short interval of his own absence, Tobiah had been allotted an apartment within the precincts of the temple of God. In fact, the great chamber which housed the meal offerings, had been prepared for him.

And to add insult to injury, the person responsible for this state of affairs was Eliashib, the high priest at that time. An old adage said, 'like priest, like people' and the high priest's behaviour probably lay behind the tolerance of the mixed multitude recorded earlier in this chapter.

It will not escape the reader's attention that the meal offering speaks of the person of the Lord Jesus Christ, and its displacement from the great chamber illustrates the Laodicean condition of the church. This condition is found where the Lord is no longer in the midst of His people, but outside seeking to gain an entrance. "Behold I stand at the door, and knock: if any man hear my voice, and open the door, I will come in to him, and will sup with him, and he with me." (Rev. 3:20) It is an invariable principle that where the Lord does not have His proper place, the enemy will gain a lodgement.

The zeal of the great reformer shone brilliantly that day against this dark and ominous background. Overwhelmed with grief, he decided his course of action. He cast forth all the household stuff of Tobiah out of the chamber. Then he commanded, and they cleansed the chambers. After that he brought in again the vessels of the house of God. And finally, he restored to its proper place the meal offering and the frankincense.

All the Tithes into the Storehouse

Another abuse then came to light. The tithe had been withheld and, as a result, the Levites had been forced out into the fields to earn their living. At the dedication, the Levites had received their regular portions and were able to engage in the service of God to which they had been appointed (Ch.12:44). But now the portions were not forthcoming and Levitical service was missing. Of course, the tithe may have been withheld as a protest against the high priest who had given Tobiah room in the house of God, but it had a profound impact upon the temple service.

Nehemiah contended with the rulers, and said, "Why is the house of God forsaken." (v.11) When he challenged the people he found a ready response for the people brought again the tithes of corn and new wine and oil and so a recovery of the situation was soon effected. And now Nehemiah appointed certain men over the important business of the Levites' support. Their chief qualification was that they were faithful men.

God's Day

The question of sabbath observance next forced itself upon Nehemiah's attention. The seventh day was being treated like any other day, even by the people of Judah who ought to have known better. In addition, traders were coming down from Tyre and finding a ready market in Jerusalem on the sabbath. Once again, as so often before, the fault lay principally with the nobles of Judah. They had evidently become indifferent to what Nehemiah described as "This evil thing that you do, and profane the sabbath day." (v.17)

Once again Nehemiah's zeal for the honour of God came to the surface. After contending with the nobles he commanded that the gates of Jerusalem should be shut before dusk and not opened again until the sabbath was past. For all that, the traders and merchants still came and waited outside the city. But Nehemiah contended with them too, and threatened to have them arrested if they persisted in that practice. They eventually got the message and stayed away until the sabbath was over. Nehemiah also laid a solemn charge on the Levites that they should cleanse themselves and come and guard the entrances to the holy city. (See also the comments in chapter 10.)

Family Life

But then a further abuse appeared that Nehemiah could not overlook. It had very far reaching implications for it concerned the nation's family life. There were at Jerusalem those who had married woman of Ashdod, of Ammon, and of Moab. The offspring of these unions greatly concerned Nehemiah, because the children spoke half in the speech of Ashdod, and could not speak in the Jews' language (v.24). When we remember that the sacred scriptures were written in the Jews' language, then the seriousness of this situation becomes immediately clear.

A whole generation might grow up with little or no knowledge of the revelation God had so wonderfully communicated to and through the chosen people. That generation would be exposed to infiltration by the evil and idolatrous influences of those pagan nations and none could forsee what the end might be. Moreover, the problem was compounded by the fact that the greatest offender was the high priest's grandson.

With quite remarkable vehemence Nehemiah contended with the people over this vital issue. He reminded them of the example of Solomon. There was no king like him, he was beloved of his God, and God made him king over all Israel. Nevertheless even Solomon sinned in this very area.

All these abuses had this in common, they flowed from the same basic source. There had been a neglect of God's word. The word of God is the great regulator of all things. It is our sole and sufficient rule in all that pertains to faith and conduct. It seems that Nehemiah, when he came back to Jerusalem called the people back again to the divine revelation that lay at the heart of their very existence as a nation.

In conclusion, we can say with conviction that this entire book and especially the final chapter highlights the power for good of an individual who is in touch with God. Singlehanded, Nehemiah stood for God and called a whole generation of his people back again to right paths. We began by saying that Nehemiah was pre-eminently a man of prayer, and we end with further proofs of that assertion. At least four times in these verses his heart is lifted in prayer to God. "Remember me, O my God, concerning this, and wipe not out my good deeds that I have done for the house of my God." (v.14) "Remember me, O my God, concerning this also, and spare me according to your great mercy." (v.22) "Remember them, O my God, because they have defiled the priesthood..." and again, "Remember me, O my God, for good." (vv.28&31)